India Ebook's

A CONCISE BOOK ON: ANCIENT, MEDIEVAL & MODERN HISTORY

Useful For UPSC, State PCS & all Competitive Examinations

India Ebook's

A CONCISE BOOK ON: ANCIENT, MEDIEVAL & MODERN HISTORY

Best Summary Book for Revision with Numorous Charts & Timelines

Useful For UPSC, State PSC & all Competitive Examinations

JANMEJOY & KRISHNA K.

INDIA EBOOK PRESS

Contents

1. Introduction to History

1.1: Historical Overview: India

The earliest evidence of humans in South Asia dates back two million years. Beginning about 30,000 years ago, stone age hunters and gatherers inhabited sites in the area. Between 8000 and 6500 B.C.E., there was a gradual shift from dependence on wild resources to domestic plants and animals.

During the period between 5000 and 2000 B.C.E., highly organized urban settlements spread throughout northern regions (present-day Pakistan and north India). Trade and communication networks linked these settlements to one another and to other distant ancient cultures.

Indus Valley Civilization and the Rise of Indo-Aryan Culture

Around **2600 B.C.E.**, regional cultures were united into a culturally integrated network in the Indus Valley region. The peoples of the region shared a number of cultural characteristics, including planned urban developments, the use of a still undeciphered script, standardized weights, and craft technologies.

The Indus Valley cultural system declined in the early centuries of the second millennium B.C.E., probably due to environmental changes in the region. Around **1500, Indo-Aryan culture** began to dominate the region. Indo-Aryan culture is associated with Sanskrit, a language related to Greek, Latin, and Avestan. The Veda--texts associated with the complex ritual system of the Indo-Aryans were composed in this period. These texts formed one important basis for religion we now call "Hinduism."

The Early and Classical Periods

At first largely nomadic, **Indo Aryan culture became increasingly urbanized and settled.** New religious orientations arose, and some of the notions associated with classical Hinduism and the other major religions of the period--such as samsara, or the notion of rebirth--developed. **Buddhism and Jainism** were founded in the middle of the last millennium B.C.E., sharing some of the basic assumptions of developing Hindu thought but critical of the hierarchical and ritual system associated with the Vedic system. Centralized power was first established on a broad scale under the Nanda dynasty in Magadha, and then expanded under the Mauryas from ca. 323-184 B.C.E.

In the **first century C.E., the Kushans**, a group of nomadic warriors from central Asia, conquered the Gandharan region of northern India, Pakistan, and Afghanistan. Smaller regional centers across the North, under Kushana control in the early centuries of the first millennium, were brought together under Gupta control in the fourth century. The **Gupta period was characterized by great flourishing of art and literature**, and is known as the "classical" period of Indian art and literature.

The "Medieval" Period

This period was characterized by the growth of strong regional centers and lack of one overarching political authority in the subcontinent. Sind in present-day Pakistan was integrated into a Muslim polity to the west; invasions by Turkic and Central Asian rulers commenced at the beginning of the second millennium C.E. Centralized powers were established, based at Delhi; independent regional kingdoms, however, continued. By the time Turkish invaders had established their power over the north as sultans, Rajput rulers in present-day Rajasthan and Punjab had established powerful small kingdoms. Regional kingdoms also flourished in the south.

The Mughals

In 1526, the Mughal empire was founded by Babur, a Turkish/Central Asian chieftain whose ancestors included Chingiz Khan an Timur. His son Humayan was driven from India in 1540 and took refuge in the court of Shah Tahmasp in Iran. Mughal rule was reestablished, and under Akbar expanded across the north. Akbar moved against Rajput rulers, who were allowed to retain control over their land in exchange for their loyalty. The Rajput hill-states of the Punjab hillswere brought under Mughal influence under the rule of Jahangir, Akbar's son.

British Rule

Although Europeans were present in South Asia as traders from the beginning of the seventeenth century, it was not until the middle of the eighteenth century that the British established rule in the region. As Mughal control waned in the eighteenth century, British power expanded. After the Battle of Plassey in 1757, the British were ceded control of the province of Bengal. By 1857, the time of the First War of Indian Independence (or, as it was known to the British at the time, the "Mutiny"), the British were poised to take control from Mughal hands permanently. Nearly two-fifths of the area, however, was left in the hands of quasi-independent rulers, who nonetheless were forced to contend with British power at the center.

2. Ancient History

It handles millions of tonnes of freight every year. The island is connected to the mainland by the **Venduruthy Bridge.**

2.1: Pre-historic Age

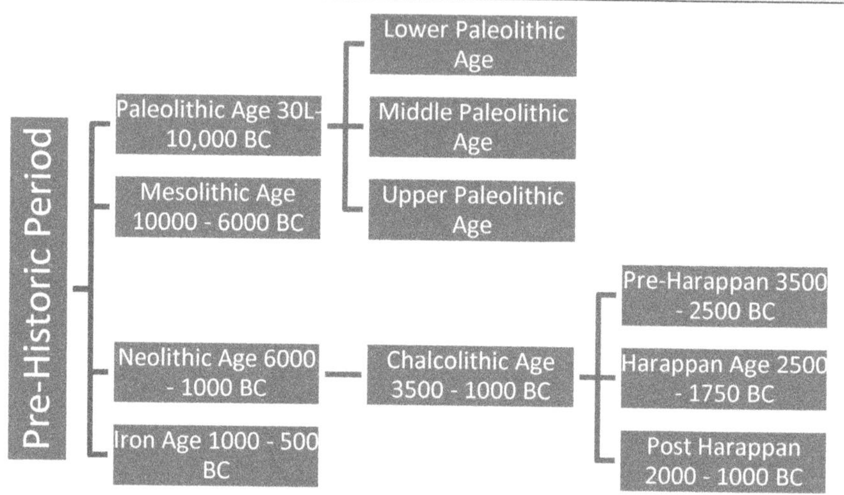

PRE-HISTORIC PERIOD (30,00,000 BCE – 600 BCE):

It consists of **five** periods - Palaeolithic, Mesolithic, Neolithic, Chalcolithic & Iron Age. **No written records** are available of this period.

Archaeological remains from this period are stone tools, pottery, artefacts, and metal implements used by prehistoric people.

Robert Bruce Foote discovered what was probably the **first Paleolithic tool discovered in India** — the **Pallavaram handaxe.**

Robert Bruce B Foote is known as the *father of Prehistoric Archaeology*.

Sir Mortimer Wheeler contributed towards our knowledge of the prehistoric cultures of India and their sequence.

PALEOLIHIC OR OLD STONE AGE (30,00,000– 10,000 BCE)

The Palaeolithic Age is the earliest period of the Stone Age, which developed in the **Pleistocene** period or the **Ice Age.**

There was **no knowledge** of agriculture, house building, pottery, or any metal.

It spread in practically all parts of India except the alluvial plains of the Indus and Ganga.

Quartzite men: Since the stone tools were made of a hard rock called quartzite, Palaeolithic men are therefore also called Quartzite men in India.

Chopper-chopping pebble culture: The implements of this culture were found first from Sohan river valley of west Punjab (Pakistan), also called as Sohan Culture.

Hand Axe culture: The implements of this culture were found first in Madurai and Attirampakkam of Madras, so also called as Madrasian Culture.

Famous sites of Old Stone Age:
- Soan valley and Potwar plateau.
- Siwalik hills in north India.
- Bhimbetka in Madhya Pradesh.
- Adamgarh Hills in Narmada Valley.
- Kurnool in Andhra Pradesh.
- Attirampakkam near Chennai.

> **Lower Paleolithic Age (5,00,000 to 50,000 BC) (Homoeractus)**

Evolution: Learned to control fire for roasting meat and warding off animals. Hunting and food gathering. Lived in trees and in caves.

Tools: Simply chopper-chopping i.e., crude and rough tools prepared out of pebbles. Choppers, Hand Axes and Cleavers.

Sites: Soan and Sohan river valley (now in Pakistan), Didwana, (Rajasthan), Hiran Valley (Gujarat), rock shelters of Bhimbetka (MP), and Belan Valley of Mirzapur (UP).

> **Middle Paleolithic Age(50,000 to 40,000 BC) (Neanderthal):**

Evolution: Language was invented in this period. Men remained hunters and food gatherers.

Tools: Flake culture: due to excessiveness of implements made from flakes. Refined and lighter tools made of harder stone material like flint were used. Diversified tools based on flakes were used, for example, blades, pointers, scrapers and borers.

Sites: Soan, Narmada and Tungabhadra river valleys, Potwar plateau (between Indus and Jehlum), Sanghao Cave (near Peshawar, Pakistan).

> ## ➤ Upper Paleolithic Age (40,000 - 10,000 BC) (Homo Sapiens):

Evolution: Other hominin species were eliminated by this time. Homo sapiens first appeared at the end of this phase. There is evidence of art in the form of paintings.

Tools: Flake-Blade culture: due to excessiveness of implements made from Flake-Blade. Even more refined and light tools. These were backed blades with two cutting edges. Blades, scrapers, and burns could be fitted in handles; Bone tools like needles, harpoons were also found.

Sites: Found in Andhra Pradesh, Karnataka, Maharashtra, Central MP, Southern UP and Chota Nagpur Plateau. Bone tools found only at cave sites of Kurnool and Muchchatla Chintamani Gavi in Andhra Pradesh.

MESOLITHIC OR MIDDLE STONE AGE: (9000 BC- 4000 BC)

This is the transitional phase between the Palaeolithic and Neolithic ages. **No snakes** are depicted in **Mesolithic Paintings.**

In India, the **credit of discovery of Mesolithic archaeological** material goes to John Evan.

Evolution: It was the transitional period between the Paleolithic and Neolithic Age. People used bow and arrow and hence, big animals were hunted down easily. First burials are reported and use of stoneornaments also appears. Domestication of animals like sheep and goats is found. The first human colonization of the Ganga Plains happened during this period.

Tools: Microlith tools i.e., tools made of micro-sized stones which were very refined. Bow and arrow and other microliths in various shapes like moon, triangular, square, rectangle, crescents and arrowhead.

Sites: Bhimbetka, Mahadaha, Sarai Nahar Rai, Adamgarh (MP), Langhnaj (Gujarat), etc. Earliest cave paintings are found at Bhimbetka (UNESCO World Heritage Site).

NEOLITHIC AGE OR NEW STONE AGE: (7000 BC - 1000 BC)

In India, the **credit of discovery of Neolithic** archaeological material goes to **Dr. Primrose.**

Neolithic revolution: V.Gordon Childe termed the Neolithic phase as Neolithic Revolution. It introduced a lot of important changes in man's social and economic life. The Neolithic age saw man turning into a food producer from food gatherer.

Man lived in huts, reared cattle, developed agriculture (wheat, barley, cotton, rice etc.), used earthenware (both handmade and wheel-made). Domestication of animals: cattle, sheep and goats was also done.

People of Neolithic age lived in rectangular or circular houses which were made of mud and reeds.

Tools: Sharper, symmetrical and polished stone tools for not only hunting but agriculture also. Daggers, digging sticks, celts, grinding stones, sickle, saw, sling-stones etc. (continuous rubbing was done to smoothen the tools).

Sites:

Kashmir valley, Chirand (Bihar), Daojali Hading, Belan valley (UP), and Maski etc.

Chopani–Mando, Belan valley: earliest evidence of use of pottery.

Burzahom: unique rectangular chopper, domestic dogs buried with their masters.

Koldihwa and Mahagara: earliest evidence of rice cultivation in the world.

South India: Maski, Brahmagiri, Hallur and Kodekal in Karnataka, Paiyampalli in TN and Utnur in Andhra Pradesh.

Koldihwa (Belan valley): presence of three-fold Neolithic, Chalcolithic and Iron Age settlements.

Mehrgarh (Pakistan): earliest Neolithic site known as the Breadbasket of Balochistan.

CHALCOLITHIC (METAL) AGE: (3500 BC-1000 BC)

The **first metal age of India** is called Chalcolithic Age. It was also called the Stone-Copper Age. Chalcolithic age is divided into **3 stages:**

- Pre-Harappan Age (3500 BC-2500 BC),
- Harappan Age (2500 BC-1750 BC) &
- Post-Harappan Age (2000 BC-1000 BC).

Chalcolithic: Chalco + Lithic was derived from the **Greek words khalkos + lithos** which means copper and stone or Copper Age.

Chalcolithic cultures had grown in river valleys. Harappan culture is considered part of Chalcolithic culture.The Chalcolithic culture corresponds to the farming communities: **Kayatha, Ahar or Banas, Malwa, and Jorwe.**

<u>Evolution:</u>
Settled & community life.
Crops cultivated were: barley, wheat, lentil, bajra, jowar, ragi millets, green pea, green and black gram and cotton.
Rice and Fish was used as food.
Technically separate but Harappan civilization evolved out of the Chalcolithic Culture.
<u>Unaware of:</u> Iron, horse and script.
Marks the beginning of use metal in place of stone yet burnt brick was generally absent.
High Child Mortality is indicated by a large number of child burials.
<u>Tools/Idols:</u>
Knives, axes, fishing hooks, chisels, pins, and rods were made of copper and its alloys.
Beads of semi-precious stones and the Terracotta image of Mother Goddess are reported.
Dead were buried in urns; at times with tools and objects.
<u>Crafts and Pots:</u>
Copper and stone tools were used simultaneously.
The chalcolithic people were expert coppersmiths. Weavers were present.
Used **Black and Red Ware**. **Painted pottery**, in black pigment; decorated with different shapes.
<u>Sites:</u>
In India it was mainly found in **<u>South-Eastern Rajasthan</u>, <u>Western part of Madhya Pradesh and Maharashtra</u>**, and in **<u>South and East India.</u>** Several bronze and copper objects, terracotta figurines and pottery were found at Paiyampalli in Tamil Nadu.
<u>Important sites:</u> Navdatoli, Jorwe, Daimabad, Ahar Banas, Malwa, Inamgaon, Songaon, Nashik, Mehgam, Kausambi, Alamgirpur, Ropar etc.

Various Chalcolithic Cultures with Sites & Features:

<u>Ahara Culture:</u> Aahar (Rajasthan), Balathal, Gilund etc. The distinctive *feature is black and red ware.*
<u>Kayatha Culture:</u> Located in **Chambal and its tributaries**, the sturdy red slipped ware with chocolate designs is the main feature.

Malwa Culture: Narmada & its tributaries in Gujarat. One of the largest Chalcolithic settlements.

Savalda Culture: Dhulia district of Maharashtra.

Prabhas & Rangpur Culture: Both of them are derived from the Harappa culture. The polished red ware is the hallmark of this culture.

IRON AGE: (1,000 BC-500 BC)

The Chalcolithic age is followed by the Iron Age. Iron is frequently referred to in the **Vedas.**

The **Iron Age of the southern peninsula** is often related to **megalithic burials**. Megalith means large stone.

The burial pits covered with these stones are extensively found in South India.

Important Megalithic Sites

Hallur and Maski in Karnataka, Nagarjunakonda in Andhra Pradesh and Adichchanallur in Tamil Nadu.

2.2: Harappan Civilization (2500-1750 BC)

The Harappan/ Indus Valley civilisation was the **first urban civilisation in South Asia**, contemporaneous with the civilisations of Mesopotamia and Egypt. It was larger than ancient Egypt and Mesopotamia civilisations.

First site excavated: Harappa site by Dayaram Sahni in 1921.

John Marshall: first scholar to use the term Indus Civilisation.

Most accepted timeline: 2500 BC-1750 BC (Carbon-14 Dating).

Period: India Civilization belongs to proto-historic period- Chalcolithic Age/Bronze Age.

Heartland of Indus Civilization: Harappa-Ghaggar-Mohenjo Daro axis.

Indus sites found in Afghanistan: Shortughai and Mundigaq.

Capital cities: Harappa, Mohenjodaro.

Port cities: Lothal, Sutkagendor, Allahdino, Balakot, Kuntasi.

Area covered: Harappan civilisation was triangular in shape and was largest among the three ancient urban civilisations, the other two being ancient Egypt and Mesopotamia (present day Iraq). It roughly covers modern day Rajasthan, Punjab, Haryana, Gujarat, and Pakistan.

Father of Indian archaeology: Alexander Cunningham, the first Director-General of the Archaeological Survey of India (ASI).

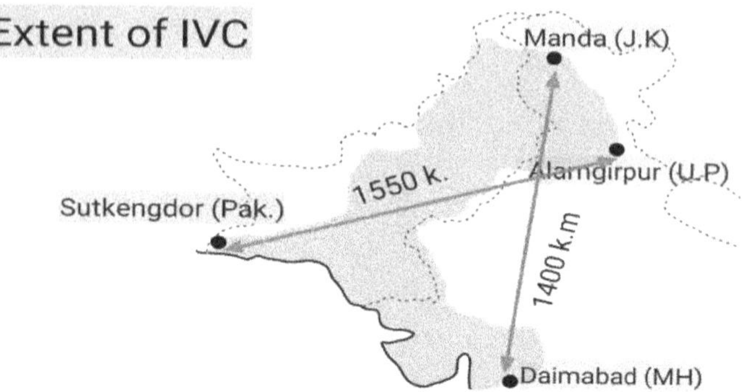

Northernmost site: Manda (Jammu-Kashmir, River: Chenab)

Southernmost site: Daimabad (Maharashtra, River: Pravara)

Easternmost site: Alamgirpur (Uttar Pradesh, River: Hindon)

Western-most site: Sutkagendor (Pakistan-Iran border, River: Dashak)

Largest site of Indus civilization : Mohenjo Daro.

Largest Indian site of Indus civilization : Rakhigarh.

Oldest script in Indian subcontinent : Harappan script.

Oldest deciphered script : Brahmi script.

Shamans are men and women who claim magical and healing powers, as well as an ability to communicate with the other world.

IMP. SITES OF IVC: LOCATION, RIVER, EXCAVATOR, FINDINGS

SITES		FEATURES
Harappa (first discovered archaeological site)	State	Pakistan (Punjab)
	River	Ravi
	Excavator	Dayaram Sahni (1921)
	Findings	Granaries, Red sandstone Male torso, Stone symbols of Lingam and Yoni, Painted pottery, Mother Goddess, Dice.
Mohenjo-daro	State	Pakistan (Sindh)
	River	Indus
	Excavator	R. D. Banerji (1922), E. Makay, Kashinath Dixit, Sir John Marshall (1930).
	Findings	Largest site of Indus civilization, Post cremation burial, Great Granary, Great Bath (largest building of civilization), Seal with Pashupathi and mother goddess, Bronze dancing girl.

Chanhudaro	State	Pakistan (Sindh), near Mohenjo-Daro
	River	Indus
	Excavator	N.G. Mazumdar (1931) and E. Makay
	Findings	Inkpot, Lipstick, Metal workers, Shell-ornament makers and bead makers shop, dog's paw imprint on brick, Terracotta model of bullock cart, Bronze toy cart.
Rangpur	State	Gujarat (Near Lothal)
	River	Madar
	Excavator	M.S. Vatsa (1931) S.R. Rao (1953-54)
	Findings	Remains of both pre-Harappan and mature Harappan culture; Yellow and gray color pots of pre Harappan people.
Lothal	State	Gujarat (Ahmedabad District, at the head of the Gulf of Cambay)
	River	Bhogava and Sabarmati river confluence
	Excavator	S Rao in 1953
	Findings	Important naval trade site, Cremation site, **Dockyard**, Granaries, Rice husk, Double burial (male female together)
Dholavira	State	Gujarat
	River	Luni
	Excavator	R Bisht in 1985 (as per NCERT). Some books mention J.P. Joshi (1990–91)
	Findings	Unique water harnessing system and its storm water drainage system, only site divided in 3 parts, Megalithic stone circle, giant water reservoirs.
Surkotada	State	Gujarat
	Excavator	J.P. Joshi (1964)
	Findings	Only site with bones of horse, Oval grave, Pot burials, Soldiers sign on potsherds.
Rakhigarhi	State	Haryana
	Findings	Largest Indian site of Indus valley civilization. Granary, cemetery, drains, terracotta bricks. Shows all three phases of Harappa Culture.

Kalibangan (Black Bangles)	State	Rajasthan
	River	Ghaggar
	Excavator	Amlanand Ghosh (1953) Dr. B. B. Lal and B. K. Thapar (1961)
	Findings	Bangle factory, **Ploughed field** surface, Camel bones, Fire altars
Banawali	State	Haryana
	River	Ghaggar
	Excavator	R.S. Bist (1973 – 74)
	Findings	**Oval** shaped settlement, Lack of systematic drainage system, Barley grains, **Lapis Lazuli**, **Fire altars**, <u>**Only city with Radial streets;**</u> Centre of pre-Harappan, Mature Harappan as well as Late Harappan civilization.
Ropar	State	Punjab
	River	Sutlej
	Excavator	Y.D. Sharma (1955–56)
	Findings	Dog buried with human oval pit burials, copper axe, **first site** to be excavated **after independence.**
Alamgirpur	State	Uttar Pradesh
	River	Hindon
	Excavator	Y.D. Sharma (1958)
	Findings	Broken copper blade, ceramic items and impression of cloth on a trough.
Daimabad	State	Maharashtra
	River	Pravara (Tributory of **Godavari** River)
	Excavator	Y.D. Sharma (1958)
	Findings	Bronze images (charioteer with chariot, ox, elephant and rhinoceros)
Kot-Diji	State	Sindh (Pakistan)
	River	Sindh
	Excavator	Ghurey (1835) Fazal Ahmed (1955)
	Findings	Bronze images (charioteer with chariot, ox, elephant and rhinoceros)

Amri	State	Sindh (Pakistan)
	River	Sindh
	Excavator	Ghurey (1835) Fazal Ahmed (1955)
	Findings	Pre-Harappan settlement; Transitional culture between pre and post-Harappan culture; Actual remains of rhinoceros, trace of jhangar culture in Late Harappan fire altars.
Suktagendor	State	Sindh (Pakistan)
	River	Dasht/Dashak
	Excavator	A Stein, George Dales
	Findings	Ash filled pot, copper axe , earthen bangles & pottery; Originally port but later cut off from sea due to coastal upliftment; Had trade links with Babylon.

PROMINENT FEATURES OF HARAPPAN CIVILIZATION

Town Planning And Structures:

➢ The towns were in a **rectangular grid pattern** with roads at **right angles**. Used **burnt mud bricks** joined with gypsum mortar (contemporary Egyptian dried bricks were used).

➢ The city was divided in two parts, the city on raised platform, known as Upper citadel & the lower town known as Lower citadel (working class quarters). <u>Fortified citadel was found</u>, **except in Chanhudaro**.

➢ Most buildings have private wells and properly ventilated bathrooms.

➢ Do not have large monumental structures such as temples or palaces for rulers unlike Egyptian and Mesopotamian Civilization.

➢ Evidence of an **Advanced drainage** system.

➢ At sites such as **Dholavira and Lothal (Gujarat), the entire settlement was fortified**, and sections within the town were also separated by walls. The Citadel within Lothal was not walled off, but was built at a height.

Agriculture:

Main crops: Wheat and Barley. Evidence of cultivation of rice in Lothal and Rangpur (Gujarat) only.

Other crops: Dates, Mustard, Sesamum, Cotton, Rai, Peas etc.

First to **produce cotton in the world** and used it for textiles, Called Sindon by the Greeks.

Used animal drawn wooden plough, and stone sickles.

Gabarbands or Nalas enclosed by dams were found but channel or canal irrigation was probably not practiced.

Produced sufficient food grains and cereals were received as taxes from peasants and stored in granaries for wages and emergencies same as Mesopotamia.

Domestication of Animals:

Animals: Oxen, buffaloes, goats, sheep, and pigs, dogs, cats, asses and camels domesticated.

Humped bulls were favored by the Harappans.

Neither **horse centered nor** were they aware of it, but evidence of horses are found in Surkotada, Mohenjo Daro and Lothal.

Lion was not known. Elephants and Rhinoceros (Amari) were well known.

Technology and Craft:

This is known as the first urbanization in India.

Along with stone, they were well acquainted with copper, silver, gold and bronze (occasionally mixed arsenic with copper instead of tin).

Iron was not known to the people.

Important crafts: spinning (Spindle whorls), bricklaying, boat-making, seal making, terracotta manufacturing (potter's wheel), goldsmiths, bead making.

They were aware of the **use of the wheel**.

Trade and Commerce:

The importance of Trade is established by the presence of Granaries, seals, a uniform script, and regulated weights and measures.

They engaged in inter-regional as well as foreign trade. Sumerian texts refer to trade relations with Meluha i.e. ancient name given to Indus region & mentions two intermediate trading stations- Dilmun (Bahrain) & Makan (Makran coast).

Used boats and bullock-carts for transportation.

No metallic money in circulation and trade was conducted by means of barter.

Import: Gold, Silver, Copper, Tin, Jade, Steatite.

Exports: Agricultural products, cotton goods, terracotta figurines, beads from Chanhudaro, conch- shell from Lothal, ivory products, copper, etc.

<u>Harappan Imports sources:</u>

Gold: Afghanistan, Iran, Kolar (South India);

Copper: Khetri (Rajasthan), Balochistan;

Tin: Afghanistan, Iran;   **Lapis lazuli:** Afghanistan;

Jade: Pamir;   **Turquoise:** Khorasan;

Steatite: Tapi Chahya (Iran);   **Lead:** South India.

Bitumen: Balochistan, Mesopotamia;

Social Organization:

Hierarchy in urban habitation. **<u>Merchants and priests</u>** were an important class of this period. Harappans were **fashion** conscious. Different hairstyles and wearing a beard were popular.

The use of cosmetics was common (Cinnabar, lipstick and collyrium)

Necklaces, filets, armlets and finger rings were worn by both men and women but bangles, girdles, anklets, ear-rings were worn by women only.

Beads were made from gold, copper, bronze, cornelian, quartz, steatite, lapis lazuli etc. naturalistic animal models as pin-heads and beads.

Polity:

Central authority may have contributed to uniform culture.

No clear idea of an organized force or standing army.

Priests did not rule in Harappa as they did in the cities of lower Mesopotamia but were possibly ruled by a class of merchants.

Religious Practices:

Seal: Male deity **<u>Pashupati Mahadeva (protosiva)</u>**, three-horned heads, and is represented in the sitting posture of a yogi, surrounded by an Elephant, Tiger, Rhinoceros, and Buffalo, and two deer at his feet. Harrapan was a **<u>predominantly secular</u>** civilization. Prevalence of the **Phallus (Lingam) and Yoni**, two deer.

Chief female deity was **<u>mother Goddess</u>**. They worshiped both male and female deities. The people of the Indus region also worshiped trees (pipal), fire and animals (unicorn, humped bull etc). Harappans believed in ghosts and evil forces. They used amulets against them.

Burials: At burials in Harappan sites the dead were generally laid in pits. Some graves contain pottery and ornaments, perhaps indicating a belief that these could be used in the afterlife.

Jewelry has been found in burials of both men and women.

Script:

Oldest script in Indian subcontinent. **Pictographic script** also found, yet to be deciphered. Writing was **Boustrophedon** - writing from right to left in one line & then left to right in the next line.

Pottery:

Plain pottery is more common than painted ware and is generally of red clay, and is uniformly sturdy and well baked.

The painted pottery is also known as Red and Black Pottery as it used red color to paint the background and glossy black paint was used to draw designs and figures on the red background.

Trees, birds, animal figures and geometrical patterns were the recurring themes of the paintings.

Most of the pottery is wheel-made. This implies they were well aware of the wheel.

Rare polychrome pottery has also been found (geometric patterns in red, black, green, rarely white and yellow).

Seals and Sealings:

Most of the seals are square shaped (2x2 square inches) made mostly from Steatite.

Seals had an animal (except cow and horse) or human figure on one side and an inscription on the opposite side or inscriptions on both the sides.

Seals were primarily used for commercial purposes, as an amulet, as a form of identification, for educational purposes as well.

Seals with symbols similar to Swastika design have also been found.

The round Persian Gulf seal found in Bahrain sometimes carries Harappan motifs.

Interestingly, local Dilmun weights followed the Harappan standard.

Art:

Bronze Casting: Practiced on a wide scale using the lost wax or Cire Perdue technique. They mainly consist of human and animal figures.

Example: Dancing Girl. She stands in a Tribhanga dancing posture.

Stone Statues: Bearded man: found in Mohenjodaro and made of Steatite, interpreted as a priest.

Red sandstone: a figure of a male torso is found in Harappa and made of Red sandstone.

Terracotta Figures: Found are less in number and crude in shape and form. Examples: Mother Goddess, mask of horned deity, toys, etc.

Weights and Measures:

Cubical weights in graduated sizes. These weights conform to the standard Harappan binary weight system that was used in all of the settlements.

DECLINE

After 2000 BC Indus Valley Civilization declined & gradually faded away. Causes of the decline of this civilization have not been firmly established.

Possible reasons – declined soil fertility, depression in land, Aryans invasion, decline of trade, Floods, Earthquake etc.

Most acceptable reason is ecological imbalance.

2.3: Vedic Age (1500-600 BC)

ARRIVAL OF ARYANS

With the advent of Aryans began the history of Vedic Period (1500 BC-600 BC). The original home of the Aryans is a debatable question and there are several views. **Aryans originally** lived in the **Steppes region**. Later they moved to central Asia and then came to the Punjab region of India around 1500 BC.

Vedic period is divided into **Early Vedic or Rigvedic** (1500 BC-1000 BC) & **Later Vedic** (1000 BC- 600 BC) periods.

The name **'Aryan'** appears in Hittite inscription (Anatolia), **Kassitte inscription (Iraq)** & Mittani inscription (Syria).

An *Iranian text*, Zend Avesta, talks about names of Aryan Gods like Indra, Varuna, etc.

Language: spoke the Indo-Aryan language, Sanskrit.

The word Veda is derived from the **root vid**, which means to know. The term **'Veda'** signifies **superior knowledge**.

The rise of Buddhism and Jainism was the direct result of this socio-economic problem arising due to Vedic Culture.

Additional Information:

- Boghazkoi Inscription:
- Mentioning four Vedic gods – Indra, Varuna, Mitra, Nasatyas– proves Central Asian Theory as their homeland.

RIG VEDIC/EARLY VEDIC PERIOD (1500 BC- 1000 BC)

The Main source of information about this age is the **Rig Veda (10 Mandalas and 1028 Hymns).**

Mandalas/Chapters from **2 to 8** are called Saptarishi Mandalas as these are composed by the seven great sages.

Mandalas 2 to 7 form the **earliest portions** of the Rigveda while 1 and 10 were latest additions.

10th Mandala has the famous Purush Sukta that describes cosmic creation (Adi Purush) along with the **4-fold** Varna System.

The **3rd Mandala**, composed by Vishwamitra, contains Gayatri Mahamantra addressed to **Goddess Savitri.**

Geographical Expansion:

Early Vedic people or Aryans settled in the land of seven rivers, called **Sapta Sindhu:** Sindhu (Indus), Vitasta (Jhelum), Asikani (Chenab), Parushni (Ravi), Bipasa (Beas), Sutudri (Satluj), and Saraswati (Ghaggar).

Their region covered present day parts of **Afghanistan, Punjab and Haryana.** Sindhu (Indus) is the most mentioned and Saraswati is the most revered (holy) river.

- **Saraswati Valley** was called **Brhmavarta.**
- The **Himalayas** were called **Himavat.**
- **Hindu Kush** was called **Munjavant.**

Society:

Rig Vedic communities comprised populations called Janas.

Society was divided into Aryans and Non-Aryans; non-Aryans were called **Dasas and Dasyus.** It was an egalitarian society. Unlike the later Vedic period, social divisions were not rigid during the Rig Vedic period. **Rig Vedic society was patriarchal.**

Basic unit of society was **family or Graham.** The head of the family was known as Grahapathi. Slaves were used for domestic purposes & not for agriculture. The term Varna is used in Rigveda with reference to Aryans & Dasa having fair & dark complexion respectively.

Women poets: Viswara, Lopamudra, Ghosha, Sikta, Nivavari, and Apala were female sages of the time and contributed to the composition of Rig Veda. Women could even attend the popular assemblies.

Child Marriage and Sati were absent and a **special widow-remarriage**, called Niyoga (levirate) was prevalent. This was done to increase the population of the **Jana**.

Two Drinks – **Soma & Sura** – Soma was sanctioned by religion & was drunk at sacrifices. Sura was disapproved by priests.

A **wealthy person was known as Gomat** and the **daughter called Duhitri** which means one who milks the cow.

Favorite pastimes: Chariot racing, horse racing, dicing, music and dance.

Monogamy was generally practiced while **polygamy** was prevalent among the royal and noble families.

Women were given equal opportunities as men for their spiritual and intellectual development. A **variety of ornaments** were used by both men and women. The **eating of cow's meat** was **prohibited** since it was a sacred animal.

Political System:

The **basic unit** of political organization was kula or family.

Rig Vedic polity was normally monarchical and the succession was hereditary. The Purohita or domestic priest was the **first** ranking official.

Janas were headed by a **Rajana** who was assisted by **Purohit, Gramani and Senani** and popular bodies like **Sabha, Samiti, Vidhata, Gana and Sardha** were present.

- **Sabha** had few chiefs while **Samiti** was a larger body.
- **Vidhata** was the oldest.

Janas were further divided into **Vis** and **Vis** in turn was divided into many **Kul or Kutumb**. **Kul** has **Griha** as its unit and Kulapa as its head while the Griha was headed by Grihapati or Dampati.

Gaun was the place where cattle were kept and Gavishthi was a quest or war for cows.

Group of Kulas made a Gram and Gram was headed by Gramani.

Vajrapati: Had authority over a large land and was leader of Kulupa & Graminis.

Rajana ruled over his people (Jana) and not over any specified area of land and hence, was called their protector (Gopa Janasya or Gopati Janasya).

There were **few non-monarchical states**, whose head was **Ganapati or Jyestha.**

Rajana had **no standing army and bureaucracy** too was absent. Military functions were performed by tribal groups called – **Vrat, Gana, Grama, Sardha.**

Tribal kingdoms: Bharatas, Matsyas, Yadus and Purus.

The **Battle of Ten Kings (Dasrajan war)** was fought on the **banks of Ravi river** for protection of wealth i.e. cow and cattle and was won by Rajana Sudas of Bharat Jana (tribe).

Right to property existed.

Rig Vedic Aryans used the coat of mail and helmet in warfare.

Economy:

Rig Vedic society was pastoral and secondary occupation was agriculture. **Cattle** was the **main form of wealth**;

Agriculture production was for consumption only. They had better knowledge of agriculture. Rigveda mentions wooden ploughshare.

Yava was the common name for any grain.

Bali was a voluntary gift from producers to the Rajana.

Trade was conducted on a barter system. In the later times, **gold coins called Nishka** were used as media of exchange in large transactions. Coins were not known.

Neither tax was imposed nor treasury was maintained.

Copper tools of this era are reported from Punjab and Haryana.

Ayas is the common name used for any metal. Gold was called Hiranya.

Aryan introduced spoked wheels.

Horses played a significant role in their life. Rig Veda has mentioned a horse-drawn chariot with spoked wheels.

Economic activities: Hunting, carpentry, tanning, weaving, chariot-making, metal smeltery etc.

Pottery type: Ochre Colored Pottery and Painted Grey Ware (PGW).

Religious Aspect:

Important Rig Vedic gods: Prithvi (Earth), Agni (Fire), Vayu (Wind), Varuna (Rain) and Indra (Thunder). Indra was the most popular.

Other important gods: Rudra, Dyaus, Ashwin, Yama and Soma.

Female gods: Aditi, Sindhu and Ushas.

Agni was regarded as an intermediary between the gods and people.

Elaborate rituals were followed during the worship.

Chanting of mantras was an important part of the ritual.

Sacrifices were practiced mainly for praja and pashu i.e. increasing population, protecting cattle, birth of male child and against disease.

Magic and Omen were not prevalent.

Maharishi Vasistha & Vishwamitra were important priests.

LATER VEDIC PERIOD: (1000 BC - 600 BC)

Sources of Information about this phase are: Sam Veda, Yajur Veda and Atharva Veda.

Other sources:

- **Brahmanas:** Detailed commentaries and explanations on the Vedas.
- **Aranyakas (forest books):** Explains metaphysics & symbolism of sacrifice.
- **Upanishads:** or books on philosophy or deeper knowledge about Aatma, Brahma etc.

They are anti-ritualistic.

The motto Satyameva Jayate written in **Devnagari** script below the profile of Lion Capital is a part of the **State Emblem of India**. It is taken from the Mundaka Upanishad.

Geographical Expansion:

Western Ganga-Valley was called 'Aryavarta'. Arabian Sea and the Indian Ocean, Several Himalayan peaks and Vindhya mountains (indirectly) are mentioned.

Growth of large kingdoms: Kuru (famous rulers: Parikshat and Janamejaya) and Panchala (popular king: Pravahana Jaivali) kingdoms. Kosala, Videha (King: Janaka; Scholar in court: Yajnavalkya) and Kasi (King: Ajatasatru) came into prominence.

Later Vedic texts also refer to the three divisions of India: Aryavarta (Northern India), Madhyadesa (Central India) and Dakshinapatha (Southern India).

Easternmost tribal kingdoms: Magadha, Anga and Vanga.

Society:

The **4-fold varna system** (Brahmins, Kshatriyas, Vaisyas and Sudras) and appearance of several jatis or castes made the social system complex.

Untouchability appeared; women's position degraded as they no longer got formal education.

Gotra was the place where **cattle resided together with 'janas'** and later developed into an identity for the janas.

Nishad, Chandala and Shabar were the untouchables mentioned. Guests were called Goghna (cow-killer).

Niyoga too was considered a **negative activity**.

Male members of the **upper three varnas** were called **dvija or twice born.** Only these were entitled to Upanayan i.e. wearing the sacred thread. Women like **Gargi and Maitreyi** accomplished in the knowledge arena; Gargi outwitted Yajnavalkya in a philosophical discourse.

Child marriages had become common. According to **Aitareya Brahmana** a daughter has been **described as a source of misery.**

Institution of Gotra & practice of gotra exogamy appeared.

Maitrayani Samhita mentions **3 evils** – liquor, women and dice.

Political System:

Janas evolved to become Janapadas. Hastinapur and Indraprastha were capitals of Kuru janapada. Frequent battles among these janapadas were fought for territory. Authority of the rajana became more evident and a support staff called ratnin; they were **12 jewels of the king,** working for rajana. Chiefship became hereditary. **Still, there was no standing army. Rajana** started **various sacrifices** like Rajsuya (consecration ceremony), Ashwamedh (horse sacrifice) and Vajpeya (chariot race).

Kings assumed titles: Rajavisvajanan, Ahilabhuvanapathi, (lord of all earth), Ekrat and Samrat (sole ruler).

Dependence on **Sabha and Samiti reduced.** Vidhata completely disappeared. Women lost their political rights of attending assemblies. Term Rashtra, indicating territory first appeared in this period. Rajana assumed titles like Samrat, Ekrat, Sarvabhouma and Virat.

Economy:

Later Vedic culture is also called **Painted Grey Ware (PGW) – Iron Phase** culture.

Iron (krishna/shyama ayas) was discovered and use of fire for clearing forest for cultivation increased.

Tin, lead, silver, Iron, gold, bronze, and copper were known to Later Vedic people.

Predominantly pastoral society of Early Vedic times had become agricultural - Wheat, Barley, Rice, Beans, Moong, Urad and Sesamum were cultivated.

Surplus produce led to **Bali and Bhaga (1/6th or 1/12th)** i.e. customary contributions (minor taxes) to the King's treasury.

Treasurer, called Samgrahitri and Bhagdukha, collected the taxes and **Vaishya were only taxpayers.**

Shataman Krishnala are believed to be coins used but have no archaeological backing; there is reference to money lending (**Satapatha Brahmana** describes a usurer as **kusidin**).

Arts and crafts: smelting, carpentry, weaving, leather-working, jewelry-making, dyeing and pottery-making, glass hoards and bangles.

Commerce and trade are indicated by mention of sea voyages.

Pottery type: Painted Grey Ware (PGW).

Religious Aspect:

Religion of early Vedic Aryans was primarily worship of nature (natural forces such as earth, fire, wind, rain and thunder) and Yajanas. **Varun and Indra**, the most important gods of **Rig Vedic age, lost prominence** in later Vedic phases. **Prajapathi** (creator), **Vishnu** (protector) and **Rudra** (destroyer) **became prominent during the Later Vedic** period.

Rituals, sacrifices and the requirement of a supervising priest (Purohita) made religious life complex. The importance of prayers declined and that of sacrifices increased. **Priesthood became a profession and a hereditary one.** There were **no temples, no idol worship.**

Magic and Omen entered the socio-religious life. At the end of the later Vedic phase Upanishadik philosophers made efforts to simplify the religious practices.

Few Kshatriyas, in Later Vedic phase, like Janak and Vishswamitra succeeded in knowing the supreme i.e. 'Brahma'. Dharma meant one's duties to oneself and to others. Rita was the fundamental law that governed the working of Shrishti (Universe).

Towards the end of this period there was a strong reaction against priestly domination and against sacrifices and rituals. The rise of Buddhism and Jainism was the direct result of these elaborate sacrifices.

VEDIC DEITIES

DEITY	INFORMATION	DEITY	INFORMATION
Indra	God of Lightning. Most Mentioned, 250 hymns, known as Purandhar or destroyer of forts. Lost prominence in the Later Vedic Phase.	Surya	God of Life Source. Had Vishnu, Savitri (Gayatri), Mitra and Pushan (vegetation, cattle-wealth and marriage) as its attributes.
Vayu	God of Air.	Marut	God of Wind.
Aditi	Mother of Gods	Usha	Goddess of Dawn
Rudra	God of Destruction. Also worshiped for healing from diseases. Merged with Shiva in the later Vedic phase.	Varun	God of Water and Morals. Most Powerful, maintained cosmic order/laws. Lost prominence in Later Vedic Phase.
Agni	God of Fire. For purity and Yajna.	Vishnu	An aspect of Surya. Least Mentioned, mentioned in 3 hymn
Prithvi	Goddess of Fertility	Aranyani	Goddess of Forest
Prajapati/ Adipurush	Supreme God. Most prominent during the Later Vedic period.	Pushan	God of the Shudras. Supposed to look after cattle.
Parjanya	God of Rain		

OFFICERS AND THEIR PROFILE IN VEDIC PERIOD

Officers	Profiles	Officers	Profiles
Vrajapati	Officer-in-charge of pasture land	Senani	Supreme commander inchief
Kshatri	Chamberlain	Jivagribha	Police official
Sthapati	Chief Judge	Gramani	Head of the village
Bhagadugha	Revenue Collector	Kulapati	Head of the family
Mahishi	Chief Queen	Spasas	Spies& Messengers
Suta	Charioteer	Madhyamasi	Dispute resolving
Takshan	Carpenter	Palagala	Messenger
Purohita	Priest of highest order	Govikartana	Keeper of Forest & Games
Akshavapa	Accountant	Sanghrahriti	Treasurer

KEY CONCEPTS

CONCEPTS	SOURCE
Gotra	Atharva Veda
Sabha and Samiti as the two daughters of Prajapati	Atharva Veda
Purusha Sukta (4-fold division of society)	Rig Veda 10th Mandala
First three ashramas (Brahmacharya, Grihasthya, Vanaprastha)	Chandogya Upanishad
Four ashrams (Brahmacharya, Grihasthya, Vanaprastha, Sanyasa)	Jabala Upanishad
Samsara (transmigration of soul)	Brihadaranyaka Upanishad
Doctrine of Trimurti	Maitrayani Upanishad
Mention of the Great Flood	Satpatha Brahamana

VEDIC TEXTS

Shrutis are the texts 'that are heard' or product of Godly revelation to the great sages (rishis) while in meditation ('dhyaan'). The four Vedas and Samhitas are included in the shrutis.

'Smritis' on the other hand are those that are recollected by normal humans. The detailed commentaries/ explanations on the Vedas (Brahmanas, Aranyakas and Upanishads), 6 Vedangas and 4 Upavedas make the smritis.

VEDIC LITERATURES

Veda	Upaveda	Brahmana	Upanishads	Aranaykas	Mantra	Priest
Riga	Ayur Veda	Aitareya, Kaushitiki Sankhyana	Aitareya, Kaushitiki	Aitareya, Kaushitiki	1028	Hotr/ Hotar
Sam	Gandharva Veda	Panchvimsh/ Tandya, Jaiminiya	Kena, Chandogya	Jaiminiya, Chandogya	1810	Udgatar
Yajur	Dhanur Veda	Taittiriya, Shatapatha	Taittiriya, Kathalsa, Brihadaranyaka	Taittiriya	2000	Adhvaryu
Atharva	Shilpa Veda	Gopatha	Mandukya, Mundaka Prashan	-	6000	Priests (Brahmins) didn't recite it.

2.4: Jainism & Buddhism

ORIGIN OF JAINISM

The **doctrine of Jaina is older** than the **Buddhist doctrine** and as old as Vedic religion. Rig Veda mentions names of **Rishabha and Arishtanemi Jain Tirthankara.**

Vishnu Purana and Bhagavat Purana describe **Rishabha** as an incarnation of **Narayana.**

Jainism does **not have a single founder**. It is commonly mistaken that Mahavir was the founder of Jainism. However, he was the last Tirthankara. Jainism came into prominence in **6th century B.C.,** when Lord Mahavira propagated the religion.

The word Jain is derived from **Jina or Jaina** - means the Conqueror. A Jina is said to possess Avadhi Jnana, (Superhuman cognition or psychic power.). All the Tirthankara were Kshatriyas by birth.

The symbol hand with a wheel on the palm symbolizes Ahimsa in Jainism. There is a word ahimsa written in the middle of it.

Additional Information:

Jain community makes for **4.5 million or 0.36 percent** of the Indian population as per **2011 census**, the **sixth** community to be designated this status as a national minority, after Muslims, Christians, Sikhs, Buddhists and Parsis. Gujarat and Rajasthan have the highest concentration of Jain population in India.

FACTORS BEHIND THE RISE OF JAINISM

Vedic religion had become highly ritualistic. It was accessible to people of all castes. The **early Jainas adopted** the Prakrit language of the common people to preach their doctrines and discarded Sanskrit language (which was mainly patronized by the Brahmanas).

Jainism offered lower people an honorable place in the society. The sacrificial ceremonies were also found to be too expensive. It accorded **equal status to women**.

The teachings of Upanishads, an alternative to the system of sacrifices, were highly philosophical in nature therefore not easily understood by all

TEACHINGS OF MAHAVIRA

Rejected authority of the Vedas & Vedic rituals. Did not believe in the existence of god. Believed in Karma & transmission of Soul.

Emphasized the equality but did not condemn the Varna system.

Advocated a life of austerity and non-violence.

Women had an equal role to play and were not looked down upon.

Man may be 'good' or 'bad' as per his actions and not birth.

Additional Information: There were 24 Tirthankara (teachers)	
1st Tirthankara	• Rishabhnath or Rishabhdev.
22nd Tirthankara	• Arishtanemi.
23rd Tirthankara	• Parshvanatha: born in Varanasi.
24th Tirthankara	• Vardhaman Mahavira.

VARDHAMAN MAHAVIRA: (539-467 BC)

Birth: Kundagrama near Vaishali. Belongs to Gnatrika Clan. Buddha and Mahavira were contemporaries.

Parents: Siddhartha (Head of Jnatrika Clan) and Trisala (Sister of Lichchhavi chief Chetaka).

Wife & daughter: married to Yashoda and had a daughter Anojja or Priyadarshana.

Teachers: Alarakama and Udraka Ramputra.

Kaivalya (highest spiritual knowledge): attained at the age of 42 under Sal tree at Jrimbhikagrama, on the bank of River Rijupalika. Henceforth, they are called Mahavir (brave), Jina or Jitendriya (one who conquered his senses), Nigrantha (free from all bonds), Arhat (blessed one), Kevalin (perfect learned).

First sermon: on the Vipula Peak at Rajgir to his 11 disciples – known as Gandharas/Gandharvas.

First disciple: Indrabhuti Gautama (female)

Death: at the age of 72 years in **c. 527 BCE at Pavapuri** near Patna.

Symbol:
➢ Mahavira's symbol was a lion.
➢ Rishabhnatha's symbol was a bull.
➢ Parsvanatha's symbol was a hooded serpent.

ROYAL PATRONS OF JAINISM

North India: Bimbisara, Ajatashatru, Chandragupta Maurya, Bindusara, Harshavardhana, Bindusara, Kharavela, Udayan, Pradyota.

South India: Kadamba dynasty, Ganga dynasty, Amoghavarsha (Rashtrakuta dynasty), Kumarapala (Chalukya dynasty).

JAIN COUNCILS

Council	Venue	Chairperson	Outcome
First 300 BC	Patliputra	Sthulabahu, Patron-Chandragupta Maurya	Compilation of 12 Angas to replace 14 Purvas
Second 512 AD	Vallabhi	Devardhigani	Final compilation of 12 Angas & 12 Upanga

PHILOSOPHY AND TEACHINGS OF JAINISM

Tenets of Jainism: Belief in God: Jainism recognised the existence of god but placed them lower than Jina (Mahavira).

It did not condemn the varna system but attempted to mitigate the evils of the varna order and the ritualistic Vedic religion.

According to **Mahavira**, a person is born in higher or lower varna as the consequence of the sins or the virtues in the previous birth. Thus, Jainism believes in transmigration of the soul and theory of Karma.

Anekantavada: Emphasizes that the ultimate truth and reality is complex, and has multiple-aspects i.e. theory of plurality. It refers to the simultaneous acceptance of multiple, diverse, even contradictory viewpoints.

Syadvada: All judgments are conditional, holding good only in certain conditions, circumstances, or senses. Syadavada literally means the method of examining different probabilities. Seven modes of prediction (Saptabhangi Nayavada).

Five Doctrines of Jainism: Parshvanatha's teachings (Chaturthi):
- **Ahimsa:** Non-injury to a living being.
- **Satya:** Do not speak a lie.
- **Asteya:** Do not steal.
- **Aparigraha:** Do not acquire property.

Mahavira added One more teaching:
- **Brahmacharya:** Observe continence.

It mainly aims at the attainment of liberation, for which no ritual is required.

Three Jewels/ Triratna: (FKA)
- **Right Faith:** Samyak Darshan – belief in Tirthankara.
- **Right Knowledge:** Samyak jnana – knowledge of the Jain creed.
- **Right Action:** Samyak charitra – practice of 5 vows of Jainism.

Two elements of the world:
- **Jiva**- meaning conscious.
- **Atma**- meaning unconscious.

Three Sources of Knowledge:
- Pratyaksha: Direct Knowledge.
- Anuman: Contemplation.
- Sayings of Tirthankara.

Five types of Knowledge:
- Mati Jnana – perception through activity of sense organs.
- Shruta Jnana – knowledge revealed by scriptures.
- Avadhi Jnana – clairvoyant perception.
- Mana Paryaya Jnana – telepathic knowledge.
- Keval Jnana – temporal knowledge.

Anuvrata: Anuvrata means the **'lesser vows'** which Jain lay-people take, as a kind of parallel to the great vows of the ascetics. They are applied to the practice of daily life.

The **five great vows** apply **only to ascetics in Jainism**, and in their place are **five minor vows** for householders. The five minor vows in Jainism are modeled after the great vows, but differ in degree and they are less demanding or restrictive than the same "great vows" for ascetics.

SECTS/SCHOOLS OF JAINISM

Jain order has been divided into **two major sects:** Digambara and Svetambara. The division occurred **mainly due to famine in Magadha** which compelled a group led by Bhadrabahu to move South India.

During the **12 years famine**, the group in South India stuck to the strict practices while the group in Magadha adopted a more lax attitude and started wearing white clothes. After **the end of famine**, when the Southern group came back to Magadha, the changed practices led to the division of Jainism into two sects.

Digambara: Monks of this sect believe in complete nudity. Male monks do not wear clothes while female monks wear unstitched plain white sarees. Follow **all five vows:** Satya, Ahimsa, Asteya, Aparigraha and Brahmacharya. Believe women cannot achieve liberation. **The earliest record of Digambara** beliefs is contained in the **Prakrit Suttapahuda of Kundakunda.**

Monasticism rules are more rigid under Digambara School.

Bhadrabahu was an exponent of this sect.

Major Sub-Sects: Mula Sangh, Bisapantha, Terapanth, Taranpantha or Samaiyapantha.

Minor Sub-Sets: Gumanapantha, Totapantha.

Svetambara: Monks wear white clothes.

Follow **only 4 vows** (except brahmacharya): Satya, Ahimsa, Asteya, Aparigraha. Believe women can achieve liberation. They believe tirthankaras can be men or women.

Svetambara tradition of Jainism indicates five eternal substances in existence: Soul (jiva), Matter (pudgala), Space (akasha), motion (Dharma) and rest (Adharma), unlike Digambaras which add the sixth eternal substance as time (Kala).

Sthulabhadra was an exponent of this sect.

Major Sub-Sects: Murtipujaka (Deravasi), Sthanakvasi, Terapanthi.

Uchche Dvd: Its promoter was Ajita Kesh Kambali. According to him, everything is destroyed after death.

Akriyavad: According to this view promoted by Puran Kasayap, there is no fruit of good and bad deeds of human beings.

Nityavad: Its promoter was Pakudha Kachaiyan. He told only seven elements, such as earth, water, fire, air, happiness, sorrow and soul (these elements do not interact with one another).

Sandehvad: Its promoter was Sanjay Beluttaputra. He neither accepted any opinion nor denied any opinion.

Sthanakvasi: It is a sect of Svetambara Jainism founded by a merchant named Lavaji in 1653 AD.

It believes that idol worship is not essential in the path of soul purification and attainment of Nirvana/Moksha. Svetambaras who are not Sthanakavasins are mostly part of the Murtipujak sect.

IMPORTANT JAIN LITERATURE

Traditionally, the original doctrine of Jainism was contained in **scriptures called Purva**. There were **fourteen Purva**. Jain literature is mainly written in **Prakrit** language.

These **Agamas** are further divided into: Angas, Mulasutra, Upangas, Prakirnaka Sutra, Chedasutra & Ulikasutras.

Kalpasutra: written by Bhadrabahu. It contains biographies of Jain Tirthankaras.

Agam or Canonical Literature (Agam Sutras): Agam ('what has come down to us' or tradition) literature consists of many texts, which are the sacred books of the Jain religion. They are written in the **Ardhamagadhi**, a form of **Prakrit language**. The canonical Jain literature is claimed to have started from **Adinatha (Rishabhnath)** (first Tirthankara).

Non Agam Literature: consists of commentary and explanation of Agam literature, and independent works, compiled by ascetics and scholars. They are written partly in Prakrit dialects (such as Maharashtri) and partly in Sanskrit.

JAIN ARCHITECTURE

Manastambha: It is found in the front side of the temple, having religious importance with an ornamental pillar structure carrying the image of Tirthankara on top and on all four cardinal directions.

Basadis: Jain monastic establishment or temples in Karnataka.

➢ Layana/Gumphas(Caves):

- Ellora Caves (Cave No. 30-35)- Maharashtra.
- Mangi Tungi Cave- Maharashtra.
- Gajpantha Cave- Maharashtra.
- Udayagiri-Khandagiri Caves- Odisha.
- Hathi-gumpha Cave- Odisha.
- Sittanavasal Cave- Tamil Nadu.

➢ Statues:

- ➢ Gomateshwara/Bahubali Statue-Shravanabelagola, Karnataka.
- ➢ Statue of Ahimsa (Rishabnatha)-Mangi-Tungi hills, Maharashtra.

➢ Jainalaya (Temple):

- Dilwara Temple- Mount Abu, Rajasthan.
- Girnar and Palitana Temple- Gujarat.
- Muktagiri Temple- Maharashtra.

SPREAD OF JAINISM

Through Sangha, it consists of women & men. Under the patronage of Chandragupta Maurya, **Kharavela of Kalinga** and the royal dynasties of south India such as the Ganges, the Kadambas, the Chalukyas and the Rashtrakutas.

When Bhadrabahu (Guru of Chandragupta Maurya) left for South India, Sthulabahu remained in the North with his followers.

Chandragupta Maurya (he himself became a Jaina ascetic and spent his last years in Karnataka).

CONTRIBUTION OF JAINISM

Preached **Non-violence** toward all living beings. Growth of **Prakrit & Kannada** language. **Vardhaman Mahavir** preached in '**Ardha-Magadhi' language**, the language of the common man.

Introduced new philosophy – **Syatvad.**

Art & architecture - statue of Gomateshwara (Shramanbdlogola), temples of Khajuraho and Abu. Tiger cave of Udayagiri and Indra Sabha of Ellora. Jainism contributed to the growth of the trading community.

TIRTHANKARAS AND THEIR SYMBOLS

Tirthankara	Symbol	Tirthankara	Symbol
Rishabhanatha	Bull	**Vimalanatha**	Hog
Ajitanatha	Elephant	**Anantanatha**	Hawk or Porcupine
Sambhavanatha	Horse	**Dharmanatha**	Thunderbolt
Abhinandananatha	Ape (Monkey)	**Santinatha**	Antelope
Sumatinatha	Heron	**Kunthunatha**	Goat
Padmaprabhu	Red lotus	**Aranatha**	Fish
Suparsvanatha	Swastika	**Mallinatha**	Jar
Chandraprabha	Moon (Crescent)	**Suvrata**	Tortoise
Suvidhinath	Dolphin	**Neminatha**	Blue lotus
Sitalanatha	Wishing Tree	**Arishtanemi**	Conch
Shreya Sanatha	Rhinoceros	**Parshvanath**	Hooded serpent
Vasupujya	Buffalo	**Mahavira**	Lion

BUDDHISM

During the later Vedic period, (around 5 circa B.C) two important religions -Buddhism and Jainism - came up with new philosophies.

PHILOSOPHY OF BUDDHISM

The religion is based upon the teachings, life experiences of its founder Siddhartha Gautam, born in circa 563 BCE.

Buddha asked his followers to avoid the two extremes of indulgence in worldly pleasure and the practice of strict abstinence and asceticism.

He ascribed instead the Madhyam Marg (Madhya Pratipada) or the middle path which was to be followed.

Roots of Buddhism in the past: Vedanta, Sankhya philosophy & Upanishad.

REASONS FOR THE SPREAD AND POPULARITY OF BUDDHISM

Liberal & democratic: Unlike Brahmanism, it was far more liberal & democratic. It won the hearts of the lower classes as it attacked the varna system.

Simple language: The **Pali** language which Buddha used was the spoken language of the masses.

Personality of the Buddha: He was kind and ego-less. His calm composure, simple philosophy and his life of renunciation drew the masses to him.

Royal patronage: Kings like **Prasenjit, Bimbisara, Ashoka, Kanishka** patronized Buddhism and helped it spread throughout India and outside as well. Ashoka sent his children to Sri Lanka for the spread of Buddhism.

Inexpensive: Buddhism was inexpensive, without the expensive rituals that characterized the Vedic religion.

CAUSES OF ORIGIN OF BUDDHISM

Expensive & complicated Vedic rituals, Superstitious beliefs, mantras confused the people. The teachings of the Upanishads were highly philosophical, therefore not understood by all.

The rigid caste system prevalent in India generated tensions in society.

Desire of Vaishya to improve their social position due to the increase in trade and economic prosperity.

Unrest in society due to supremacy of the Brahmins. Practice of killing cows became a hindrance to the new Agricultural economy.

GAUTAMA BUDDHA (563 BC-483 BC)

He is also known as Siddharta, Sakyamuni & Tathagata. Belonged to the Sakya Clan.   **Father: Suddhodana.**

Mother: Mahamaya (princess of the Kosala dynasty); brought up by his maternal aunt, Prajapati Gautami. She gave him the name 'Gautama'.

Wife: Yashodhara and had a son, Rahula.

Birth Place: Lumbini, Kapilavastu (in present Nepal) capital of Sakya republic.

Teachers: Alara kama and Udraka Ramputra

Enlightenment: At age of 33 under Peepal tree at Uruvela (Bodhgaya) on banks of river Niranjana (Falgu).

First Sermon: Sarnath (Deer park) (Varanasi) to 5 disciples including Mahakasyapa (first disciple); known as Dharma Chakra Parivarthana (turning of the wheel of law).

Maha-parinirvana: Under Sal tree at Kushinagar (in UP) at age of 80. Idea of renunciation:Sight of Sick man, Old man, Corpse and Ascetic.

Contemporaries of Buddha: Mahavira Jaina, Kings Prasenjit, Bimbisara and Ajatasatru.

IMPORTANT CONCEPTS RELATED TO BUDDHISM

Doctrine of Buddhism: Did not involve himself in debates of soul & Brahma but concentrated on worldly problems.

Buddhism accepts transmigration and impermanence.

Buddha did **not believe in God or soul**. **Stressed on karma and ahimsa**. Against the varna system. World is full of sorrows & people suffer on account of desires.If desires are conquered,

Nirvana will be attained & there will be freedom from the cycle of birth & death.

Literary Sources:

Ceylonese Chronicles: Mahavamsa by Mahanama, Dipavamsa and Attakatha by Wattagamani.

Tibetan Chronicles: Divyavadana-Kalachakra.

Tripitaka/ Three baskets of Buddhist scripture:
- **Sutta Pitaka:** Sutra related to Buddha and companions.
- **Vinaypitaka:** monastic rules.
- **Abhidhampitaka:** Doctrine and philosophy of Buddhism.

Jataka Folklore: stories related to the birth of Buddha/in Chinese they are called Sadok.

Milindapanha: Questions of Milinda i.e Greek king Meander and answers of Buddhist monk Nagasena.

3 Jewels of Buddhism (Triratna):
- Buddha: Founder/Teacher.
- Dhamma: Teachings.
- Sangha: Order of Buddhist monks/nuns.

Three Pitakas:

Vinaya Pitaka: consists of rules of conduct and discipline applicable to the monastic life of the monks and nuns.

Sutta Pitaka: consists of the main teaching or Dhamma of Buddha. It is divided into five Nikayas or collections: Digha Nikaya, Majjhima Nikaya, Samyutta Nikaya, Anguttara Nikaya, Khuddaka Nikaya.

Abhidhamma Pitaka: philosophical analysis and systematization of the teaching and the scholarly activity of the monks.

Other important Buddhist texts include **Divyavadana, Dipavamsa, Mahavamsa, Milind Panha** etc.

4 Noble Truths: 'Chatwari Arya Satyani'

Truth of Suffering (Dukkha): Buddha taught that everything is suffering (Sabbam Dukkham). It refers not only to the actual pain and sorrow experienced by an individual, but also to the potential to experience these things.

Truth of the cause of Suffering (Samudaya): Suffering is part of living. Desire (Trishna) is the main cause of suffering.

Truth of the End of Suffering (Nirodha): This suffering can be ended by attaining Nirvana/ Nibbana.

Truth of the Path Leading to the End of Suffering (Astangika-Marga): There is a path that leads to the end of suffering.

5 Buddha's Teachings (Panchshila):

Buddha also established code of conduct both for the monastic order and the laymen to follow which are also known as the **Five Precepts or Panchshila:**

- No killing and respect for life.
- Abstention from theft.
- Abstention from sexual misconduct.
- Abstention from falsehood.
- Abstention from intoxication.

The Five Aggregates (Pancha-khanda or Panch skandha):

Buddha believed that a human being is a collection of Five Aggregates and a proper understanding of these is an essential step towards the attainment of freedom from suffering.

Material Form (Rupa): It includes the five physical organs (ear, eye, tongue, nose & body) and the corresponding objects of the sense organs (sound, sight, taste, smell and tangible objects).

Feeling or Sensation (Vedana): The aggregate of feelings arising out of contact with the objects of the senses is of three kinds-pleasant, unpleasant and indifferent.

Perception (Sanna): This aggregate is the capacity to recognize & conceptualize things by associating them with other things.

Mental formation (Santharas): This aggregate may be described as a conditioned response to the object of experience.

Consciousness (Vinnana): The aggregate of consciousness is an indispensable element in the prediction of experience. It is essential to understand that consciousness depends on the other aggregates and does not exist independently.

Eight-Fold Paths (Astangika Marga):

The path consists of various interconnected activities related to knowledge, conduct, and meditative practices. **Eight-Fold Path** is more about unlearning rather than learning:

Right understanding (Samma-Ditthi): Understanding that the Four Noble Truths are noble and true.

Right thought (Samma-Sankappa): Determining and resolving to practice Buddhist faith.

Right speech (Samma-Vaca): Avoiding slander, gossip, lying, and all forms of untrue and abusive speech.

Right conduct (Samma-Kammanta): Adhering to the idea of nonviolence (ahimsa), as well as refraining from any form of stealing or sexual impropriety.

Right means of making a living (Samma-Ajiva): Not slaughtering animals or working at jobs that force you to violate others.

Right mental attitude or effort (Samma-Vayama): Avoiding negative thoughts and emotions, such as anger and jealousy.

Right mindfulness (Samma-Sati): Having a clear sense of one's mental state and bodily health and feelings.

Right concentration (Samma-Samadhi): It signifies 'Samadhi' in the sense of enlightenment or Buddhahood.

GREAT EVENTS IN BUDDHA'S LIFE AND SYMBOLS

Great Events in Buddha's Life	Symbols
Avakranti (conception or descent)	White Elephant
Janma (birth)	Lotus & Bull
Mahabhinishkramana (Great Renunciation)	Horse
Nirvana/ Sambodhi (enlightenment)	Bodhi Tree
Dharmachakra Parivarthana (first Sermon)	Wheel
Mahaparinirvana (Death)	Stupa

BUDDHIST SANGHA AND ITS FEATURES

The oldest prayer place in history where slaves, Insolvents, and diseased were not allowed. There were **64 types of crimes** called Pathimokshas, which were prohibited. **Women were also allowed to join**.

Important Buddhist Scholars:

Moggaliputta Tissa: launched Ashoka's dhamma campaign.

Asvagosha: wrote Buddhacharita and Sanskrit drama Sariputra Prakarana (Sariputra - the disciple of Buddha).

Nagarjuna: Founded Madhyamaka school of Mahayana Buddhism, gave theory of Sunyavada-Emptiness and important work including Mulamadhyamakakarika.

Buddhaghosa: most important commentator of Theravada, important work is Visuddimagga.

Dharmakirti: Teacher at Nalanda, called as Kant of India.

Asanga and Vasubandhu: Two brothers who flourished in the Punjab region in the fourth century CE.

Asanga was the most important teacher of Yogacara or Vijnanavada school founded by his guru, Maitreyanatha.

Vasubandhu's greatest work, Abhidharmakosa, is still considered an important encyclopedia of Buddhism.

Dinnaga: The last mighty intellectual of the fifth century, also well known as the founder of the Buddhist logic

Bodhisattvas:

In Mahayana, Buddhism Bodhisattva is a person who can reach nirvana but delays doing so through compassion for suffering beings.

It is similar to the concept of incarnations in Hindu Mythology. Bodhisattvas are common figures in Buddhist literature and art.

Bodhisattva	Traits
Maitreya	**Future Buddha** & earliest bodhisattva. Also known as **Ajita-Bodhisattva**. Holds a waterfall in his left hand. Popular laughing Buddha is claimed to be an incarnation of Maitreya.
Samantabhadra	Universal Bodhisattva. Associated with Meditation. Manifestation is action.
Vajrapani	Like Indra, holds a thunderbolt (depict power). Depicted as one of the 3 protective deities around Buddha. Others two: **Manjusri** and **Avlokiteshwara**.

Bodhisattva	Traits
Avalokitesvara	Kind-hearted. Manifests Buddha's compassion.
Kshitigarbha	Guardian of purgatories and children. Bodhisattva of hell-beings or earth immortal beings.
Amitabha	Buddha of Heaven.
Sadaparibhuta	Manifests never disparaging spirit.
Manjushri	Stimulator of **understanding** and he holds a book describing **10 paramitas.** Depict male Bodhisattva wielding a flaming sword in his left hand.
Akasagarbha	He is boundless as space. Manifestation of wisdom.

BUDDHIST COUNCILS

Councils	Venue	Chairman	Patron
1st – 483 BCE	Sattapani cave at Rajgriha	Mahakasyapa	Ajatasatru (Harayanka)
	Outcomes: It was held soon after the Mahaparinirvan of the Buddha. The council was held with the purpose of preserving Buddha's teachings (Sutta) and rules for disciples. During this council, the teachings of Buddha were divided into three Pitakas. Compilation of Sutta pitaka and Vinaya Pitaka by Upali		
2nd – 383 BCE	Vaishali	Sabakami	Kalashoka (Shishunaga)
	Outcome: Division into Sthaviradins & Mahasanghikas.		
3rd – 250 BCE	Pataliputra	Mogaliputta Tissa	Ashoka (Maurya)
	Outcome: Compilation of Abhidhamma Pitaka. Decision to send missionaries to various parts of the world.		
4th – 98 CE	Kashmir	Vasumitra & Vice-chairperson: Ashvaghosa	Kanishka (Kushana)
	Outcomes: Compilation of Mahavibhasha sastra. All deliberations were conducted in Sanskrit. Division of Buddhism into Hinayana (the Lesser Vehicle) and Mahayana (the Greater Vehicle). Abhidhamma texts were translated from Prakrit to Sanskrit.		

Buddhist Universities with their Location and Founder

University	Location	Founder
Nalanda	Bihar	Kumargupta I (Gupta Ruler)
Odantapuri	Bihar	Gopala (Pala Ruler)
Bikramshila	Bihar	Dharmapala (Pala Ruler)
Somapuri	North Bengal	Dharmapala (Pala Ruler)
Jagadal	Bengal	Rampala (Pala Ruler)
Vallabhi	Gujarat	Bhattrika (Maitrak Ruler)

MAJOR SCHOOLS: MAHAYANA & HINAYANA

Mahayana Buddhism:

The term Mahayana (Sanskrit word) which literally means Greater Vehicle. Sought salvation through grace & help of Buddha & Bodhisattvas.

It originated in northern India and Kashmir and then spread east into Central Asia, East Asia and some areas of Southeast Asia: China, Mongolia, Korea, Tibet and Japan.

Believed that Buddha will be born again. **Worship** Buddha in **idol** form.

Language: Sanskrit.

Mahayana sects include: Pure Land, Zen, and Vajrayana (or Tantric) Buddhism.

Sub-schools: Chittmatra & Madhyamaka.

Zen is a sub school of Mahayana which is prevalent in China, Korea and related to Taoism.

Hinayana Buddhism:

Considered a Lesser Vehicle. Also known as Abandoned Vehicle or Defective vehicle. It believes in the original teaching of Buddha or Doctrine of elders.

- Orthodox, conservative schools of Buddhism.
- Followed the original teachings of Buddha.
- Sought individual salvation through self-discipline & meditation.
- **Buddha will never be reborn.**
- Did not believe in Idol worship.

Language: Pali.

Buddha was an intellectual, not a god.

Encompasses **18 sub schools**. Most important: Sarvastivada, Theravadin & Sautantrika. Buddhism preached by **Emperor Ashoka** was Hinayana.

Other Schools: Theravada, Vajrayana & Zen

Theravada Buddhism is older and the more conservative of the two main divisions of Buddhism and is often referred to as the 'Tradition of the Elder'. **Theravada is a Hinayana** sect.

Theravada Buddhists strive to become Arhats and gain freedom from the cycle of samsara.

Sarvastivadin considers everything empirical to be impermanent, they maintain that the dharma factors are eternally existing realities.

Theravada Buddhism developed in **Sri Lanka** and subsequently spread to the rest of Southeast Asia. It is the dominant form of religion in Cambodia, Laos, Myanmar, Sri Lanka, and Thailand.

Vajrayana means The Vehicle of the Thunderbolt, also known as Tantric Buddhism.

This Buddhist school developed in India around 900 CE.

Believed in acquiring magical power for liberation.

Developed in Tibet and believes in the worship of female deities - Taras.

It became popular in Eastern India, particularly Bengal and Bihar.

Zen: It is a sub-school of Mahayana Buddhism that originated in China during the Tang dynasty as the Chan school of Chinese Buddhism and later developed into various schools.

It spread to Japan in the 7th century C.E.

Meditation is the most distinctive feature of this Buddhist tradition.

Important Terms and Meanings Related to Buddhism

TERM	MEANING	TERM	MEANING
Arhats	Liberated beings	Nirvana	State of Supreme bliss
Pavarana	Assembly at the end of Vassa	Mahabhini shkramana	Great going forth – renunciation.
Posadha	Restoration of vows	Chaityas	Prayer halls of monks
		Viharas	Monasteries
Sheel	Refers to when a layperson leaves home to live the life of a Buddhist renunciate among a community of bhikkhus		
Sarma	One who labors, toils, or exerts themselves (for some higher or religious purpose) or a seeker, who performs acts of austerity, ascetic.		
Upasampada	Refers to the rite and ritual of ascetic vetting (ordination) by which a candidate, if deemed acceptable, enters the community as Upasampada (ordained) and authorized to undertake ascetic life.		
Vassa	Three-month annual retreat observed by Theravada practitioners. It lasts for three lunar months, usually from July to October (wet months).		
Uposatha	It is a Buddhist day of observance. The Buddha taught that the Uposatha day is for the cleansing of the defiled mind, resulting in inner calm and joy.		
Parajika	Literally meaning defeat, it included four most serious offenses involving expulsion from the Sangha		
Upasakas	**Male followers** who have taken refuge in the Buddha, Dhamma & Sangha, but who have not taken monastic vows.		
Upasikas	Female followers who have taken refuge in the Buddha, Dhamma and Sangha, but who have not taken monastic vows.		

CONTRIBUTION OF BUDDHISM

Socio-Religious Sphere	Art and Culture Sphere
Stressed on **ethical living** rather than rituals, animal sacrifices, etc.	The stupas at **Sanchi, Bharhut** and **Gaya**, the chaityas and viharas.
Does **not recognize the existence of God/soul.**	<u>Promoted education</u> through residential universities like those at Taxila, Nalanda and Vikramasila.
Taught the **Middle path** for salvation.	
Propagated Liberal & democratic values **Women were given equal status** as men.	The language of **Pali** and other local languages developed through the teachings of Buddhism.
<u>Opposed caste and Varna</u> system, any form of hierarchy and discrimination.	
Authority of Vedas was challenged. Faith was given a rational basis.	
Concept of <u>ahimsa</u> was its chief contribution.	Promoted the **spread of Indian culture** to other parts of Asia.

CAUSES FOR THE DECLINE OF BUDDHISM

Decline of Buddhist Sanghas due to violation of Buddhist principles & discipline. The Buddhists began to **adopt Sanskrit**, the language of the elite. So the masses moved away. The <u>**attack of Huns in 5th & 6th centuries**</u> and **Turkish** invaders in the **12th century** destroyed the monasteries.

Buddhism was **mainly an urban religion** with rural India always Hindu. When Islam came to India, it impacted the urban regions & thus Buddhism was impacted.

Revival of Brahmanism and division among Buddhists.

Rajput rulers were warlike and could not follow the policy of Ahimsa.

Loss of Royal Patronage.

Image worship was started in Buddhism by the Mahayana Buddhists.

UNESCO's Heritage sites related to Buddhism:

- Archaeological Site of Nalanda Mahavira at Nalanda, Bihar.
- Buddhist Monuments at Sanchi, MP.
- Mahabodhi Temple Complex at Bodh Gaya, Bihar.
- Ajanta Caves, Aurangabad, Maharashtra.

Heritage City Development Scheme (HRIDAY) and identification of 3 Buddhist circuits are some of the few initiatives by the central government to harness the Buddhist pilgrims to both augment the Tourism and employment opportunities.

2.5: Pre-Mauryans Period (600-300 BC): 16 Mahajanapadas, Magada Empire

AGE OF MAHAJANAPADAS

The sixth century BCE is known as an era of Second Urbanisation in the Indian Subcontinent.

The center of economic and political activity shifted from the North-West, Punjab, Haryana, and Western UP, to Eastern UP and Bihar (Ganga Basin).

According to Buddhist texts, Anguttara Nikaya (land between Himalayas and Narmada) was divided into 16 independent states (Mahajanapadas).

It was the phase during which Janapadas became greater in size and got involved in expansion of territory resulting in the formation of Mahajanapadas.

Sources of information: Anguttara Nikaya (Buddhist texts) and Bhagwati Sutra (Jain texts).

Magadha displayed the tendency and potential of becoming an empire. This period of Indian history was deeply influenced and driven by development of philosophical movements like Jainism and Buddhism.

THE SIXTEEN MAHAJANAPADAS

Mahajanapadas were either monarchical or republican:

Monarchies: on the Gangetic plain – Magadha, Kosala, Vatsa, Aanti, Anga, Kashi, Gandhara, Shursena, Chedi and Matsya.

Republics: on the foothills of the Himalayas and in north- western India – Malla, Vajji, Kamboja and Kuru.

Economic growth led to development of urban centers and first use of coins is also reported from this period; they were called punch-mark coins. **Large scale** use of **iron tools**, spread of agriculture and North Black Polished Pottery is also associated with this age.

During this period **'Brahmi' script appeared** for the <u>**first time**</u>.Taxation added to the wealth of the state, prostitution too appeared in the cities.

Mahajanapadas	Capital	Some Facts
Kamboja	Pooncha/Rajpura	Laid in Afghanistan & Some parts of Jammu & Kashmir. The kambojas were famous for their excellent horse breeds.

Gandhara	Taxila	Extended up to the Kabul valley. Gandhara king Pukkusati exchanged gifts with Bimbisara in Magadha and went on foot to see the Buddha. According to the Greek historian **Herodotus**, Gandhara formed the twentieth province of the Achaemenid empire of Persia.

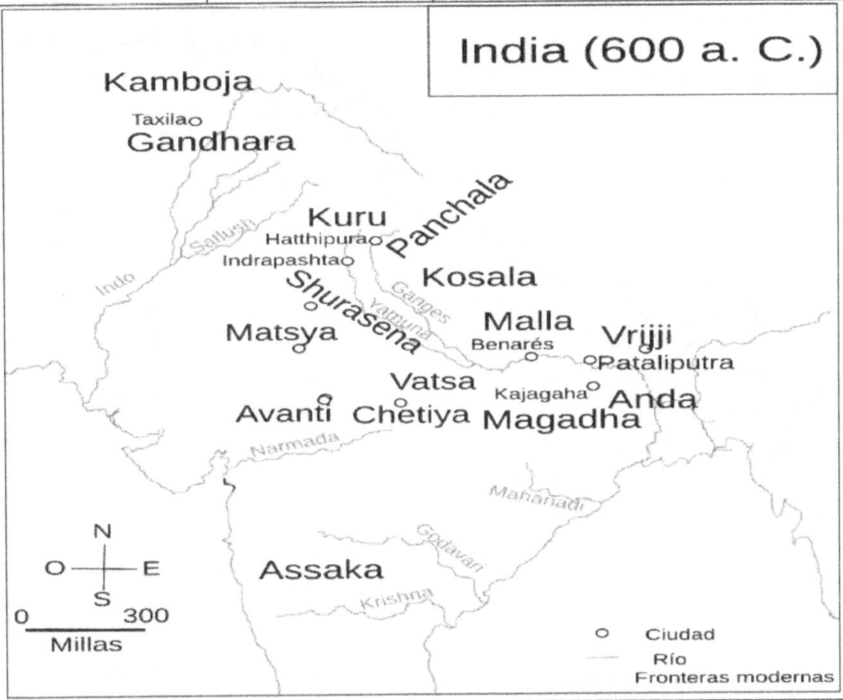

Ashmakas	Paithan	Situated on the banks of the river Godavari near modern Paithan in Maharashtra. It was the only Mahajanapada situated to the south of the Vindhya Range, and was in Dakshinapatha.
Vatsa	**Kaushambi**	Central Malwa and the adjoining areas of Madhya Pradesh. The Vatsa capital is located 64 km from Allahabad at Kaushambi on the bank of the Yamuna. Swapna Vasavadatta was written about king Udayana (ruler of Vatsa) love affairs.

Avanti	Ujjaini (N)/ Mahishmati (South)	The Avanti's king Pradyota is famous in legends, and had relations with Udayan, the ruler of Vatsa.
Shurasena	Mathura	It was marked by uneven roads, excessive dust, vicious talks and 'Yakshas'. Belonging to the Yadava clan which is also associated with Krishna.
Chedi	Suktimati	Eastern parts of Bundelkhand and adjoining areas.
Malla	Kusinara/ Pava	Non-monarchical, Kusinara is identified with Kasia in Gorakhpur district and Pava is possibly identical with Pawapuri in Patna district.
Kuru	Hastinapur/ Indraprastha	Delhi-Meerut region. Tribal polity. Formed because of the alliance and merger between the Bharata and Pura tribes.
Panchala	Ahichhatra (W.Panchala), Kampily (S. Panchala)	Modern Kampil in Farrukhabad district. Tribal polity.
Matsya	Virat Nagri	Associated with modern Jaipur- Bharatpur- Alwar region of Rajasthan.
Vajji (Vrijji)	Vaishali	From north of the Ganga and up to as far as the Nepal hills. A confederation of eight clans (atthakula), of whom the **Videhans**, the **Lichchhavis**, the **Jnatrikas** and the **Vrijjis** were the most important. A flourishing non-monarchical state in the time of Mahavira and Gautama Buddha.
Anga	Champa	Modern districts of Munger and Bhagalpur, Bihar. Noted for its wealth and commerce.
Kashi	Banaras	Initially, the most powerful of them played an important part in the subversion of the Videhan monarchy. Leading center of textile manufacture in the time of the Buddha; the kashaya (orange brown) robes of the Buddhist monks are said to have been manufactured here.

Koshala	Shravasti	**Ayodhya** on the Saryu, **Saketa** adjoining it and **Shravasti** (modern Sahet-Mahet) on the borders of the Gonda and Bahraich districts of Uttar Pradesh, were three important Koshalan cities.
Magadha	Rajagriha/ Girivraja	Modern Patna and Gaya districts of Bihar; bounded on the north and west by the rivers Ganga and Son respectively. Did not follow the varna system, hence Brahmanical texts make derogatory remarks for Magadha and Buddhist text hold it high in regard as being the place of Buddha's enlightenment (Gaya). Details of the king and people of Magadha are mentioned in the **Anguttara Nikaya.**

SOCIO-ECONOMIC SURVEY OF MAHAJANAPADA PERIOD

Economy:

Most urban settlements were inhabited by merchants and artisans (organized into a **'sartha' guild**).

Practice of **trade and crafts** was **hereditary**.

Most important cities of the time were settled on the banks of the rivers and trade routes.

Money economy: Trade was facilitated through use of money called 'Nishka' and 'Satamana' (mentioned in Vedic texts; no archaeological evidence).

Mahajani System (banking system): Buddhism and Jainism recognized Mahajani or money lending.

Agriculture was made easier with the use of iron tools. Paddy transplantation was practiced. Barley, cotton, pulses, millets and sugarcane were also produced.

1/6th of the farm produce was to be paid to the royal agent as tax and there were no intermediate landlords.

Rich peasants were called **'Grihapatis'.** Vessa meant Merchants Street.

'Balisadhakas' collected the compulsory taxes called 'bali' from peasants and Vaishyas only.

Land route: A route led from Taxila to north Afghanistan and Iran and from there silver, gold, Lapis lazuli, jade (ornamental mineral) were obtained as raw materials.

Sea route: The Pali texts of this period throw light on foreign trade. There is a mention of sea merchants in the Angutar Nikaya.

Two major trans-regional routes of the time:

Uttarapatha: of northern India, stretching from the north-west across the Indo-Gangetic plains to the port city of Tamralipti on the Bay of Bengal.

Dakshinapatha: of southern India, stretching from Patliputra in Magadha to Pratishthana on the Godavari, and connected to ports on the western coast.

Society:

The **Pali texts (Vinay Pitaka)** suggests **three types of villages (grama).**

Typical villages: inhabited by various castes and communities – headed by gramabhojaka, gramini or gramakas.

Suburban villages: which were in the nature of craft villages.

Border villages (anamika-grama): which were situated on the periphery of the countryside.

Society was divided into **four** varnas: Brahmans, Kshatriyas, Vaishyas and Shudras.

Writing had started and was used for book keepings in trade, taxation and the large size of the army.

Lower varnas were subjected to many **discriminations.**

The **strengthening of patriarchal** control within the household led to the increased subordination of women. **Position of women** degraded further except in Buddhist and Jain orders.

Number of castes appeared and the condition of untouchability further worsened.

The age of **marriage of women was reduced** compared to the **Vedic** period. Severe punishments were awarded by royal agents.

Administration and Army:

Jatakas or stories of previous lives of Buddha mention that land grants were given in favor of great religious leaders.

The **King was the highest administrative official** who was supported by other officials called Mahamantras who performed functions of

Mantrin (minister) and Senanayaka (Commander), judge and chief accountant etc. Another class of officers performing similar functions were called **Aayuktas.**

Administration of the village was under a village headman called Gramabhojaka, Gramini or Gramika.

Large, professional and permanent army.

This period marks the origin of the Indian legal and judicial systems. The civil and criminal law was based on the varna division.

THE MAGADHA EMPIRE

The Magadha word was **first mentioned** in **Atharva** veda. Kashi, Koshala, Magadha and the Vajji **confederacy—remained significant** in the **6th century BC.**

Jarasandha, who was a descendant of **Brihadratha** (eldest of the five sons of Vasu, the Kuru king of Chedi) founded the empire in Magadha. Magadha emerged victorious and became the center of political activity in north India. **Magadha had a strategic position** between the upper and lower part of the Gangetic valley.

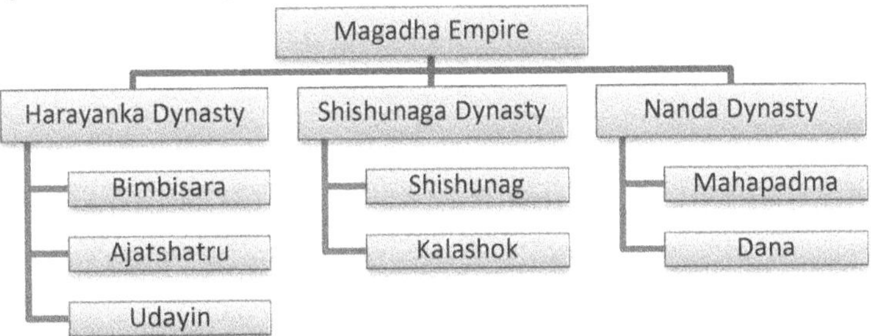

The **iron ores** in the hills near **Rajgir** and **copper and iron deposits** near **Gaya** were the natural assets of Magadha. **Capital of Magadha: Rajgriha.** First King of Magadha was Brihadratha and he belonged to the Brihadratha dynasty.

During the **reign of Bimbisara and Ajatasatru**, the prosperity of **Magadha reached its zenith.**

HARYANKA DYNASTY (544 BC-492 BC)

> **Bimbisara (542-493 BC)**

The **first important ruler** of Magadha, Bimbisara, was a **patron of Buddhism.** He was a **contemporary** of **both Buddha and Mahavira**, and paid equal respect to them.

Bimbisar's capital: Rajgriha or Girivraja. He is described as **Seniya**, i.e., the one 'with an army'.

Started the practice of using **matrimonial alliances** to strengthen his political position. **Dynastic marriages** promoted goodwill between Bimbisara and contemporary rulers of Koshala and Viji.

Policy of conquest and expansion. **First king to have a standing army.**

Bimbisara sent his personal physician **Jivaka to Ujjain** to win the friendship of **Pradyota, the king of Avanti.**

Bimbisara's aggression was towards **Anga Mahajanapada**, it was **annexed** to Magadha. Effective and excellent administrative system.

> ### Ajatashatru (492-460 BC)

Ajatashatru killed his father - Bimbisara - and ascended the throne.

Adopted expansionist policy & **defeated Koshala** and **Vaishali.**

Ajatashatru was the **contemporary of Buddha.** Buddha died during his reign. He was most powerful and aggressive ruler.

He convened the First Buddhist Council at Rajgriha just after the death of Buddha in **483 BC.**

Used two innovative military weapons: War engine (Mahashilakantaka); Chariot with mace (**Rathamusala**). He done **fortification of Rajgriha.**

> ### Udayin (Udayabhadra) (460-444 BC)

As per the Mahavamsa, the Sri Lankan Buddhist chronicle, Ajatashatru's son Udayin succeeded Ajatashatru and ruled for the next sixteen years.

Founded the **new capital at Pataliputra** (modern Patna), situated at the confluence of **Ganga and Son** rivers.

The last ruler of the Haryanka dynasty. Succeeded by **three kings:** Aniruddha, Manda, Nagadasaka. They were later succeeded by the Sisunaga dynasty.

SHISHUNAGA DYNASTY (412 BC-344 BC)

> ### Shishunaga

Shishunaga was earlier a **Viceroy/Amatya** (high ranking official) at **Varanasi (Banaras).** Temporarily shifted capital to **Vaishali.**

During the reign of Shishunaga, Magadha annexed **Avanti (Ujjain)** and many other Janapadas into the fold of the Magadha empire.

> ### Kalasoka

Also known as Kakarvarna (according to the Puranas). Son and successor of Shishunaga. Kalashoka shifted the capital back to Patliputra. Convened the Second Buddhist Council held at Vaishali.

Nanda Dynasty (First non-Kshatriya dynasty) (344 BC-323 BC)

➤ Mahapadma Nanda

Mahapadma Nanda, who was from a shudra (non-Kshatriya) lineage, laid the foundation of the Nanda dynasty in Magadha. Also called **Ugrasena** in Pali texts, because of his large army. He is called the <u>**first historical emperor of India.**</u> Puranas refer to him as <u>**destroyer of all Kshatriyas**</u> i.e. Sarvaksatrantaka and Ekarat.

Presence of **Jain ministers like Kalpaka, Sakatala, etc.** in his court indicates his **leaning towards Jainism.**

➤ Dhana Nanda

Last important king of the **Nanda dynasty**. He is referred to as <u>**Agrammes or Xandrames**</u> in Greek texts. Credited with the invention of Nandopakramani (a particular measuring standard).

He was a **contemporary of Alexander of Macedon**. Alexander invaded North-Western India during his reign. **Finally,** he was overthrown by **Chandragupta Maurya** along with Chanakya, which led to the foundations of the Mauryan Empire in Magadha.

CAUSES OF MAGADHA'S SUCCESS

Magadha enjoyed an <u>**advantageous geographical**</u> position. Magadha was located on the **main land route** between west and east India. Both **Rajagir** and **Pataliputra** were located on **strategic positions** (near to richest Iron ores). The area had <u>**fertile soil**</u> drained by **river Ganga,** which received enough rainfall.

Pataliputra has a famous <u>**water fort (Jaladurga)**</u>, encircled by rivers on <u>**three sides**</u>, the **Ganga, Son & Gandak** making the region impregnable to enemies and **fourth river Ghaghra** joins the Ganga nearby.

Magadha had <u>**huge copper and iron**</u> deposits. Magadha could easily control trade because of its strategic location. It had a large population which followed different occupations such as agriculture, mining, building cities and served in the army. With the <u>**annexation of Anga**</u> by **Bimbisara, river Champa** was added to the Magadha Empire. Champa was important in trade with South-East Asia, Sri Lanka and South India.

Magadha society had an <u>**unorthodox character**</u>. **Society was not much dominated by the Brahmanas.** It had a good <u>**mix of Aryan and non-Aryan**</u> people.

<u>Emergence of Jainism and Buddhism</u> led to a revolution in terms of philosophy and thoughts. They both enhanced liberal traditions.

Magadha had strong standing armies and availability of iron enabled them to develop advanced weaponry. Magadha was the first to deploy elephants on a large scale in wars.

FOREIGN INVASIONS

> **Iranian (Persian) Invasion in India**

Founder of the <u>**Achaemenid empire of Persia**</u> (Iran), **Cyrus II** invaded the region west of river Indus, **during Bimbisar's reign** in Magadha, and succeeded in <u>**establishing control over Gandhara, Kamboja, and Madra.**</u> His grandson **Darius I** conquered <u>**Punjab**</u> and <u>**Sindh**</u>.

As a result, Indo-Iranian trade, influences of language, art and architecture increased. **Bell-shaped capital**, Ashokan inscriptions and introduction of **Kharosthi script** are the products of this influence.

> **Greek/Alexander's Invasion (327 BC – 325 BC)**

After defeating **Darius III**, the last Achaemenid emperor, <u>**Alexander crossed the Hindukush**</u> and entered northwestern India which was an Achaemenid province in **327 BC**.

<u>**Ambhi (Omphis)**</u>, the king of **Takshashila,** submitted to Alexander.

Battle of Hydaspes (Jhelum):

Porus, who ruled the territory between the <u>**Jhelum and the Ravi**</u>, was defeated and captured after **initial resistance**. <u>**Alexander**</u>, impressed by **Porus' resistance**, reinstated him to power.

Alexander's army **refused** to **cross river Beas (Hyphasis)** to fight further and thus a clash between the tired Macedonian mercenaries and the huge army of the Nandas did not happen. After establishing a few Greek settlements in north-west India, <u>**Alexander died in 323 BC**</u> in **Babylon.**

Impacts:

Direct contact between India and Greece (Europe). Encouraged political unification of north India under the Mauryas. Accounts by Alexander's historians provide information about that period.

Seeds of Indo-Bactrian and Parthian States in India.

Greek influences on the Gandhara School of Art and Architecture.

New land & sea routes were discovered by Alexander.

2.6: Mauryans Period

The Maurya period not only marks the establishment of the first sub-continental empire, but also the development of innovative and comparatively stable governance strategies.

Maurya ruled over the whole of the sub-continent, except Kerala, Tamil Nadu, and some parts of northeastern India.

SOURCES OF INFORMATION

Literary Sources

> **Megasthenes' Indica:**

Contains information about the Mauryan administration, particularly the administration of the capital city of Pataliputra and also the military organization. It throws light on contemporary social life.

> **Kautilya's Arthashastra:**

Written by Kautilya, a contemporary of Chandragupta Maurya, most important literary source for the history of the Maurya. Kautilya was also called **Indian Machiavelli.** The manuscript of Arthashastra was first discovered by **R. Shama Sastri in 1904.**

> **Visakha Datta's Mudra Rakshasa:**

Drama in Sanskrit which describes how **Chandragupta with the assistance of Kautilya overthrew the Nandas** (written during the Gupta period). It also gives a picture on the **socio-economic condition** under the Mauryas.

> **Buddhist Text:**

Jatak Stories, Dipavamsa, Ashokavadana, Divyavadana.

Trinity of Buddhist texts: Mahavamsa, Milindapanho, and Mahabhashya.

> **Brahmin Literature:**

Puranas reveal the lists of Mauryan kings and the chronology.

Hemachandra's **Parishishta Parvan.**

Dandin's **Dashakumaracharita.**

Banabhatta's **Kadambari.**

Archaeological Sources

> Punch marked coins, Northern Black Polished Ware (NBPW).
> Wooden palace of Chandragupta Maurya in Pataliputra.
> Ashokan inscriptions and Edicts.
> Junagarh Inscription of Rudradaman I.

THE MAURYAN DYNASTY

The founder of the Mauryan dynasty, **Chandragupta Maurya (324/321 – 297 BCE)** inherited a large army of the Nandas, which he used to conquer almost the whole of north, the northwest, and a large part of the peninsular India. There is a **lot of ambiguity** about the **origins and caste of the Maurya family**, and they vary from text to text.

Buddhist texts: Digha Nikaya, Mahavamsa, and Divyavadana, speak of the Mauryas as belonging to a Kshatriya Moriya clan associated with the Shakyas.

Brahmanical sources: consider them Shudras and heretics.

Chandragupta Maurya (322–298 BC):

Chandraupta or **Sandrokottos** (referred to in Greek literature) launched a series of wars against **Dhana Nanda.** Laid the foundation of **Mauryan empire in 322 BC** with help of **Chanakya (Kautilya)**.

Credit for the first unification of North India is attributed to Chandragupta Maurya. He was the **chief architect** of the Mauryan empire and built a vast empire, which included Bihar, Nepal, western and north-western India, and the Deccan.

In **305 BC**, Chandragupta defeated **Seleucas Nikator**, the Greek king after Alexander. **Megasthenes (wrote the Indica)**, a Greek ambassador, was sent by Seleucus in the Chandragupta Maurya court.

According to **Jaina sources**, **Chandragupta embraced Jainism towards the end of his life** and abdicated the throne in favor of his son.

Accompanied by Bhadrabahu, a Jaina saint, he **went to Shravanabelagola (Karnataka)** (famous for the statue of Gomateshwar), where he died by slow starvation (Sallekhana).

Bindusara (298–273 BC):

Chandragupta was succeeded by his son Bindusara, known to the Greeks as Amitrochates, while the Mahabhasya refer to him as **Amitraghat** (the destroyer of foes). Madrasar, Simhasena are other names used for Bindusara. Bindusara followed the **extreme fatalistic order (religion) Ajivika** founded by Makhali Gosala.

This order had complete disregard for karma. **Greek sources** also mention his **diplomatic relations** with western kings.It is believed to have joined the Ajivika sect.

Tibetan Buddhist monk Taranatha describes Bindusara as conqueror of the land between two seas i.e., peninsular India.

Divyavadan, Buddhist biographical narrative of Mauryan Kings, mentions a revolt at Taxila being suppressed by Ashoka (son of Bindusara); who was Kumara or viceroy of Ujjain at that time.

Ashoka the Great (273–237 BC):

Ashoka was **crowned in 269 BC**. Radhagupta, helped Ashoka in usurping the throne. Regarded as one of the greatest kings of all times, and probably was the **first ruler** to maintain **direct contact with his people** through his inscriptions. He was appointed the **viceroy of Taxila and Ujjain** during the reign of **Bindusara.**

Other names of emperor:
 - Buddhashakya and Ashoka (in the Maski Edict),
 - Dharmasoka (Sarnath inscription),
 - Devanampiya (beloved of the gods), and
 - Piyadassi (pleasing appearance, given in the Sri Lankan Buddhist chronicles Dipavamsa and Mahavamsa).

His capital was at **Pataliputra (Patna)** and had **provincial capitals** at **Taxila** and **Ujjain**.

Childrens of Ashoka: Mahendra/Mahinda and Sanghamitra/Sanghamitta.

8 years after coronation, Ashoka fought the horrible **Kalinga War in 261 BC.** Ashoka was moved by the untold miseries caused by the war, renouncing conquest by warfare, in favor of cultural conquest. In other words, Bherighosha was replaced with Dhammaghosha.

Under Ashoka, almost entire subcontinent came under single control except extreme south: Uttarapatha (Taxila), Avantirashtra (Ujjain), Prachi (Pataliputra), Kalinga (Toshali) and Dakshinpatha (Suvarnagiri) were important provinces.

Ashoka was **not an extreme pacifist**. He retained Kalinga and incorporated it into his kingdom; he also did not disband the army.

Under Ashoka, the **Mauryan Empire reached its climax.**

Contributions of Ashoka

 - **Ashoka and Buddhism:**

He became a Buddhist under the guidance of Mogaliputta Tissa. Ashoka is known for his Dhamma policy.

Ashoka convened the Third Buddhist Council at Pataliputra in 240 BCE, in order to strengthen the Sangha. It was presided over by Moggaliputta Tissa.

According to tradition, and as mentioned in the Mahavamsa and Dipavamsa, he was converted to Buddhism by his nephew Nigrodha.

He visited Bodhgaya, and organized missions. He appointed special officers called Dharma Mahamatras to speed up the progress of Dhamma.

Buddhism for the first time went outside India during his reign. He sent his son Mahendra and daughter Sanghamitra to Ceylon (Sri Lanka).

➤ Ashoka's Dhamma:

The concept of non-violence and other similar ideas of Ashoka's Dhamma are identical with the teachings of Buddha.

His policy of dhamma was a broad concept with elaboration of a way of life, signifying a general code of conduct and a set of principles to be adopted and practiced by the people at large.

4-cardinal points of Dhamma: Tolerance, Nonviolence, Good Conduct (Obeying parents and elders, respecting Brahmanas and Monks) & Welfare.

A new officer called, Dhamma mahamatra was appointed for promotion of Dhamma.

➤ Ashoka Rock Edicts:

James Princep, a *British* antiquary and colonial administrator was the **first person to decipher** Ashoka's edicts.

The national emblem of India is taken from the Ashoka's Sarnath Pillar.

Name of Ashoka occurs only on minor rock edicts. He was the first king to speak to people directly through inscriptions.

Rock and pillar edicts:

Major and minor rock edicts (16 and 2 respectively).

Major and minor pillar edicts (17 and 3 respectively).

Features of pillars:

Mostly, the pillars are similar in form and dimensions

- Two types of stones are used:
- Spotted white sandstone (from Mathura).
- Buff coloured sandstone and quartzite (from Amaravati)

Mostly monoliths (i.e., carved out of a single piece of stone) and have a lustrous, polished surface.

Do not have a base, and the plain, smooth cylindrical shaft tapers slightly upwards.

Have a bell capital (a stone carved in the shape of an inverted lotus).

On top of the bell capital is a platform (abacus) which is intended to support the crowned animal.

Places of pillars: Kandahar (Afghanistan), Khyber Pakhtunkhwa (Pakistan), Delhi, Vaishali and Champaran (Bihar), Sarnath and Allahabad (Uttar Pradesh), Amaravati (Andhra Pradesh), and Sanchi (Madhya Pradesh).

Eastern part of the empire: Magadhi language in Brahmi script is used. (Magadhi is the dialect of Prakrit found in Magadha).

Western parts of the empire: Prakrit in kharosthi script is used.

Kandhar Inscriptions is bilingual, it uses **Greek and Aramaic** languages and scripts.

Major Rock Edict XIII contains an extract in Greek and Aramaic as well.

Principles of Dhamma were clearly stated in Edicts. Summed up as follows:

- Service to father and mother, practice of ahimsa, love for truth, reverence to teachers and good treatment to relatives.
- Prohibition of animal sacrifices and festive gatherings and avoiding expensive and meaningless ceremonies and rituals.
- Efficient organization of administration in the direction of social welfare and maintenance of constant contact with people through the system of Dhamma Yatra.
- Humane treatment to servants by masters and prisoners by government officials.
- Consideration and non-violence towards animals and courtesy to relations and liberality to Brahmins.
- Tolerance among all the religious sects.
- Conquest through Dhamma instead of through war.

Major/Minor Rock Edicts

Edict No.	Message
I	**Prohibits animal slaughter.** Only two peacocks and one deer were killed in Ashoka's kitchen. He wished to discontinue this practice of animal slaughter.

II	**Planting medicinal herbs and humans and animals** were given medical treatment. Also mentions about the **Cholas**, the **Pandyas**, the **Satyaputra** and the **Kerala Putras.**
III	**Pradeshikas, Rajukas** and **Yuktas** going on tours of inspection, preaching dhamma.
IV	**Dhammaghosa** replaced **Bherighosha** (war drum).
V	About **Dhamma Mahamattas'** appointment.
VI	Mantri Parishad & officers like Pulisani & Pativedakas (reporters).
VII	**Religious tolerance** in his own kingdom and in the neighboring kingdoms.
VIII	**Dhamma Yatras** (dharma tours) replaced **Vihara-Yatras** (Royal pleasure tours).
IX	Emphasis on **dhamma** and **moral conduct.**
X	No desire for fame and glory by the king.
XI	**Policy of dhamma** is the best policy to follow and a best gift.
XII	Appeals tolerance amongst all sects and people to honor the dhamma of others. Also mentions about **mahamattas in charge of women's welfare** (Ithijika Mahamatta).
XIII	**Ashoka's victory over Kalinga.** Victory of Ashoka's Dhamma over Greek Kings, Antiochus, Ptolemy, Antigonus, Magas, Alexander and Cholas, Pandyas etc. This is the **Largest Edict.** It mentions Kamboj,Nabhaks, Bhoja, Andhra etc.
XIV	Describes engraving of inscriptions in different parts of the country.

Minor Rock Edicts

These Edicts are concentrated in the South & Central parts of the empire. They highlight the personal **history of Ashoka** and the summary of **Dhamma.**

The edict found at **Kandahar is bilingual**, being inscribed in **Greek and Aramaic** and Minor Rock Edict III (Bairat) is addressed to the Buddhist clergy. The title most commonly adopted by Ashoka in his edicts is **Devanampiya Piyadassi** (beloved of the Gods).

SOCIO-ECONOMIC SURVEY OF MAURYAN PERIOD

Mauryan Economy:

Sources of revenue: the revenues came from land, ferry tax, forests, mines and pastures, license fee from craftsmen and fines collected in the law courts.

The **land revenue** was normally fixed as **one-sixth** of the produce.

Occurrences of famines are also reported in Kautilya's Arthashastra and Jaina texts.

Tolls were also levied on commodities brought to town for sale.

Crown land was called **Sita.**

The Mauryan State had a strict legal and penal system (civil and criminal); tax evaders attracted the death penalty.

Punch-marked coins (mostly silver) were used for transactions.

Hired laborers were called **karmakaras.**

State monopoly of mining, forest, salt, sale of liquor, manufacture of arms and metallurgy.

Mauryan Society:

Society was clearly divided into a **four-fold Varna** system, **slavery (Dasa) existed** in the society. There was **improvement** in the social status of **Vaishyas and Shudras.**

There is **no mention** of either **Varna or Sati** in the **Ashokan edicts.**

Varna-Shankar Vivah or inter-varna or intercaste marriages too are reported; these were of two kinds, namely, Anuloma (groom of higher varna/caste) and Pratiloma (bride of higher varna/caste).

While **Kautilya mentions 9 categories** of slaves, **Megasthenes** reports **its absence.** As per the **Jataka tales** untouchables like Chanadala, Nishad, Shabar etc. existed and were treated inhumanely.

Women's position in society deteriorated severely: widow remarriage stopped, the institution of Ganikas (prostitution) expanded.

Mauryan Administration:

The Mauryan Empire was divided into **5 provinces:**

Uttarapatha (Capital: Taxila),   Avantipatha (Ujjain),

Dakshinpatha (Suvarnagiri),   Prachyapatha and   Magadha.

Huge army and Navy were maintained in which all the 4 varnas were allowed to serve.

The ascendancy of the Mauryas had resulted in the triumph of monarchy in India.

Central Administration:

Council of ministers (Mantriparishad): consisted of Purohita, Mahamantri, Senapati and Yuvaraja to assist the king in administrative matters.

Highest officers were called 'Tirthas' and 'Adhyakshas' (superintendents), they managed **26 departments**.

Census: Census was conducted regularly during the Mauryan period Judicial and Police departments: Kautilya mentions presence of both civil and criminal courts.

➤ Important Officials:

Mantri – Chief Minister.

Mantriparishad/Adhyaksha – Head of Council of Ministers.

Purohita – Chief priest.

Senapati - Commander-In-Chief.

Yuvaraj - Crown Prince.

Samaharta - Revenue Collector.

Shulkadhyaksha - Officer-In-Charge of Royal Income.

Spies (gudda purushas) and informers (prativedakas) played an important role.

Local Administration:

The Mauryan state also had local and municipal administration; Vish or Ahara (districts) were the units of a province.

Megasthenese's account mentions 6 committees of five members each for administering the municipalities.

➤ Important Officers:

Sitadhyaksha: Supervised agriculture.

Panyadhyaksha: Superintendent of Commerce.

Yukta: Subordinate Revenue Officer.

Pradeshika: Chief revenue officer.

Sthanika: Head of local administration. worked under Preadesika

Rajuka: Revenue settlement officer.

Sams Adhyaksha: Superintendent of market.

Pauthavadhyaksha: Superintendent of weight & measure.

Nava Adhyaksha: Superintendent of ships.

Sulkaadhyaksha: Collector of tolls.

➤ Village Level Officers:

Gramika: Head of the village.

Gramvriddhas: Panchayat consists of Village elders to settle disputes.

Sudarshan lake (Girnar Hill, Gujrat) was constructed during the reign of Chandragupta Maurya.

Tamralipti (Tamlook in Midnapur, WB) in the east and Bharuch/Broach (Gujrat) in the west were two important ports.

Raja (the king), Mitra (Friend), Durg (fort), Amatya (the secretaries), Janapada (territory), Kosha (the treasure), Sena (Army) were the 7 elements of states of Kautilya's Saptanga theory.

OFFICERS IN MAURYAN STATE

Officer	Position	Officer	Position
Prashasti	Prison Head	Koshadhyaksha	Treasury Officer
Sannidata	Treasury Head	Vyabharika	Chief Judge
Nayaka	City Security Chief	Koshagar Adhyaksha	Royal Treasury Manager
Dandapala	Head of Police	Kunyadhyaksha	Officer of Forest
Durgapal	Head of Royal Fort	Karmantika	Head of Industries & Factories
Annapala	H/o Food Grains Dept	Man Adhyaksha	Office of Time & Place Determination
Rajjukas	Land Measurer	Lauhadhyaksha	Metallurgy Officer

DECLINE OF THE MAURYAN EMPIRE

Over-centralisation, cumbersome bureaucracy, super heavy taxation (on almost every activity) and foreign invasions were main factors of decline.

Neglect of North: West frontier and construction of great wall of China.

Financial Crisis: Ashoka incurred huge expenditure for promotion of his 'Dhamma Mission'.

Over-tolerant, non-violent attitude killed the fighting spirit of the army.

After Ashoka's death in **232 BC** Mauryan emperors were incompetent and oppressive.

Pushyamitra Shunga, a Mauryan army commander, killed the last Mauryan emperor Brihadrath and founded the Shunga Dynasty in 187 BC.

2.7: Post-Mauryans Period: Sunga, Satvahana, Kanvas, Indo-Greeks, Saka, Parthian, Kushan

The **Maurya rule** thus <u>came to an end</u> and the **Sunga Dynasty** was established as the ruler of **Magadha**.

The native dynasties like <u>**Shungas, Satvahana, and the Kanvas**</u> ruled in eastern India, central India and the Deccan region.

Foreigners like <u>**Indo-Greeks or Bactrians**</u>, <u>**Sakas**</u>, <u>**Parthians**</u> and the <u>**Kushanas**</u> ruled in north-western India.

This was a period defined by the intermingling and influence of new cultures, vibrant doctrinal debates, the rise in devotional worship of images and the institutionalization of religious activity.

The period also saw the emergence of sophisticated sculptural and architectural styles.

SOURCE OF INFORMATION

Puranas; Dharmashastra; Manusmriti also known as <u>**Manav Dharma Shastra**</u> is composed by Sage Manu and is the <u>**first detailed law-book**</u> available.

Gargi Samhita and the **Mahabhashya** of <u>**Patanjali**</u>(commentary on <u>**Panini's Ashtadhyayi**</u>).

Buddhist Jatakas, Divyavadana, Mahavastu and the Milindpanho (Sanskrit, Milindaprashna).

Malavikagnimitram of Kalidasa and the **Harshacharita** of Banabhatta.

Periplus of the Erythraean Sea written by an anonymous Greek seafarer (pattern of trade between India and the Western world).

Epigraphic records in **Kharosthi** found in large numbers in **Gandhara** and **Central Asia** refer to different facets of **India's** regular contacts with these regions.

SHUNGA DYNASTY (187 BC-78 BC)

<u>**Founder:**</u> Pushyamitra Sunga, who was the commander- in-chief under the Mauryas. <u>**Capital at Pataliputra**</u> and a second capital at <u>**Vidisha**</u> (under son Agnimitra's viceroy).

> **Pushyamitra Shunga:**

He defended the country (the Gangetic valley) and its culture against foreign invasions (**Greeks**).

Pushyamitra shunga erected **Bharhut stupa.**

He followed **Brahmanism** and performed two Ashvamedha sacrifices.

Also promoted the growth of Vaishnavism and the Sanskrit language.

> ➤ **Agnimitra:**

After Pushyamitra, his son Agnimitra ruled.

Kalidasa's play **Malvikagnimitra** is a **love story** of the King Agnimitra and a handmaiden Malvika.

A significant attempt at penetrating into India by **Demetrius I** of Bactria was countered successfully by Vasumitra, son of Agnimitra.

Performed **Ashwamedh** sacrifice for revival of Brahmanical order and patronized scholars like Patanjali and Manu.

> ➤ **Vasumitra:**

After Agnimitra, Vasumitra became the King and was succeeded by **7 more** kings of the same dynasty.

Shunga's empire covered regions of Bihar, Bengal and Uttar Pradesh and northern Madhya Pradesh. The last ruler of the Shunga dynasty was **Devabhuti.**

Importance of Shungas

Shungas issued gold and silver coins and they inherited and continued with the Mauryan structure of administration.

They patronized the Brahmanical order, yet there was no antagonism towards Buddhism.

Mathura school of art achieved new heights, especially in realistic human depiction.

Manu's Manav Dharma Shastra or **Manusmriti** and Kalidasa's Malavikagnimitram are said to have been composed during this period.

Yavanarajya inscription, Dhangadeva-Ayodhya inscription mentions Shungas.

Nanaghat inscription, **Nasik** Inscription, **Hatigumpa** inscription of Kharavela, **Erragudi** inscription of Ashoka provide important information about Shungas.

SATAVAHANA DYNASTY

Satavahana are referred as **Andhras** in the **Puranas Simuka** was the founder of the Satavahana dynasty. The **Satavahana kingdom** is chiefly composed of modern-day Andhra Pradesh, Telangana and Maharashtra.

At times, their rule also included parts of Karnataka, Gujarat and Madhya Pradesh.

Primary capital: Pratishthana (modern Paithan in Maharashtra) on Godavari river & second Capital was Amravati.

Sources of Information: Aitareya Brahmana, Puranas, epics, Brihat Katha of Gunadya, Kamasutra of Vatsyayana.

The Satavahana graves are reported to be encircled by big pieces of stone and therefore they are known also as megalithic people.

Next important king was **Gautamiputra Satkarni** (known as Ekabrahmana) whose achievements are recorded in the Nasik inscription of Gautami Balashri (his mother). He defeated Sakas, Greeks, Parthians and Nahapana (king of western Satrapa)

Around **150 CE**, Rudradaman took advantage of weak successors of Gautamiputra Satkarni and defeated them.

At the end of **2nd CE**, another important ruler **Yajnasut Alakrni** came to the throne who conquered back the areas of Gujrat, Malwa and Andhra.

After Alakarni, Satavahana power declined and they were replaced by Vakataka Dynasty in the sameregions, who too were Brahmins.

SIGNIFICANCE OF SATAVAHANA RULE

➢ **Political Setup and Administration**

Important officials: Amatyas, Mahamatya, Mahasenapati.

King: upholder of Dharma.

Feudal traits can be seen in their administration.

Practice of **tax-free land grants** to **Brahmins.**

Amatyas and Mahamatras were district officers during Satavahana rule which was called as **Ahara.**

Gaulmika administered the **rural areas.**

Katakas and Skandhvaras were the **military camps.**

Dharmshastras not only set ideals for the people but also for the King.

➢ **Art and Architecture**

Satvahanas promoted development of architecture in hills of the Western Ghats where caves were cut in Ajanta, Nasik, Kaule, Bhaja, Kondain, Kanheri.

These caves were cut in to make Chaityas (Buddhist cave-temple) and Viharas (Buddhist rest houses). Karle Chaitya is the largest cave temple.

Nagarjunkonda and **Amravati** were important centers of trade and art. Stupas were constructed here, <u>use of white marble</u> too is reported for the **first time.**

Contributed to the development of **Ajanta school of painting** which is known for beautiful color combinations, drawings, expression of emotions, and spirituality.

Buddha's entire life is pictured - Saptashati.

Gatha sattasai: excellent work in Prakrit by **Hala**

➢ Economy:

Did not issue gold coins but issued gold as bullion.

They issue coins of lead, potins (silver-like alloy used in coins. It is typically a mixture of copper, tin and lead), copper etc.

Trade with the <u>**Roman empire**</u>.

Pratishthana & Tagara were important trade centers.

They were the first native rulers to issue their own coins with the portraits of the rulers.

Paddy transplantation, cotton production and exploitation of iron ores (Karimnagar and Warangal) was commonly practiced.

➢ Society and Religion

Being matrilineal, most of the kings are named after their mother- Gautamiputra Satakarni, Vasisthiputra Pulumayi, Yagnasri Satakarni.

With the flourishing of Mahayana Buddhism, worship of Krishna and Vasudeva was also common.

They supported both Buddhism and Brahmanism although they were Hindus and claimed Brahmanical status.

➢ Literature

Most of the inscriptions of the Satavahana rulers are in Prakrit Language as it was their official language.

Satavahana ruler Hala, himself a great scholar, composed Gathasaptasati.

INDO-GREEKS (200 BCE-100 BCE)

Indo-Greeks were the Greek people who got settled in India and became localized over a period of time.

Indo-Greek rule in India had <u>**3 branches**</u>, namely, **Bactria** i.e., North Afghanistan, **Taxila** (Takshashila) and **Sakal or Sialkot** which is now in Pakistan.

An ambassador from the Taxila branch, Heliodorus was sent to the court of the King of Vidisha. Heliodorus got a stone pillar constructed in Greek style (different from Ashokan style) which was dedicated to Lord Vasudeva.

Demetrious and Menander or Milind are two significant rulers mentioned from the Sakal or Sialkot branch of Indo-Greek. Menander or Milind (165 BC-145 BC) adopted Buddhism under Nagasen who wrote Milindpanho in Sanskrit. This book is a great source of history of this age.

Indo-Greeks were the first to issue gold coins bearing inscriptions of images of Kings and Gods. India learned the use of the curtain (yavan) from Greeks.

The Greek term horoscope was derived from the term Horasastra. They introduced the practice of governorship.

Growth of metallurgy, medicine, astronomy, stonecutting, perfume-making are evidence of technical advancements under Indo-Greeks.

Patronizing both Buddhism and Hinduism, the greatest contribution of Indo-Greeks is witnessed in the development of Gandhara School of Art.

Gandhara School of Art:

In this, Greek techniques are applied over Buddhist themes and it is also known as Greeko-Buddhist Art.

Taxila, Peshawar, Bactria, Bamiyan, Hadda; in Afghanistan; Baigram (Kashmir) were important sites of development of this school of art.

Muscular body, beard and mustache are seen in the images of Buddha and Bodhisattvas. Images of Greek gods and Kings too are reported.

Use of gray sandstone, outer robe (Roman influence), facial images and anthropomorphic (human form) God (Greek influence) is evident in the Gandhara School of Art.

Significance of the Indo-Greeks:

1st rulers to issue **coins** as well as **gold coins.**

They inscribed date & human figures on the coins.

Many coins have been found with **images of Indian deities** also.

Also introduced drama/play with use of curtains.

Patronized Buddhism, most of the Indo-Greek kings were Buddhists.
Greek influence is mostly seen in art and sculpture, particularly the Gandhara School of Art.

PARTHIANS

At the **end of 100 BC** few kings with **Iranian** names like Pahlavas of IndoParthians, captured **north-western India.**

In the **reign of Gondophares** (the most significant of the Indo-Parthians) St. Thomas is said to have come to *India* for the **propagation of Christianity.**

SAKAS/ SCYTHIANS

Sakas who were also known as Scythians, were from **Western China.**

The **first Shaka king** was **Maues or Moga** (approx **80 BC**) who is known from inscriptions and a series of coins.

Mathura, Ujjain and **Girnar** were **centers of Saka** rule in north India.

They ruled in the capacity of **Satrapas (i.e., governors) and Mahasatrapas.**

With control over western Ganga valley, parts of central India and Gujarat, **Sakas were** almost always **at war with Satavahana** and put pressure over the Deccan region.

Rudradaman(130-150CE) of Ujjain center of Sakas is of significance as he finds mention in **Junagarh inscription.** This inscription is in **Sanskrit** unlike previous Prakrit inscriptions.

Rudradaman got the **lake Sudarshan repaired** for better irrigation (constructed during the time of Chandragupta Maurya).

Huge numbers and a great variety of **silver coins** are reported from western India that are attributed to the Sakas.

Patronizing Indian art and culture many of the Saka rulers got themselves Indianized.

Important centers of development of art were Sanchi, Mathura and Gandhara.

The **King of Ujjain** defeated Sakas and assumed the **title of Vikramaditya** and established the Vikram Samvat or era in 58 CE.

KUSHANS

Kushanas (or Yueh-Chis) too were from China, they ruled in North-West India with Purushpur (Peshawar) as their capital.

Kanishka, a **Mahayan Buddhist,** was the most important Kushana ruler. **Wem Kadphises, Huviska** and **Vasiska** were other important Kushana rulers in India.

The **4th Buddhist council** at <u>**Kundalvan Vihar (Kashmir)**</u> with Vasumitra as president was held during Kanishka's reign. Ashwaghosh was **vice-president** of the Mahayana Buddhist council.

Adopted the title of **'Devputra',** and has been shown wearing a 'peaked helmet' on some coins.

<u>**Buddha Charita**</u> (biography of Buddha), was composed by **Ashwaghosh** of Patliputra.

Nagarjuna was a great scholar of his court, who propounded the <u>**Madhyamika Philosophy**</u> of **Mahayana Buddhism.** Nagarjuna also discussed the *idea of relativity* and hence was called as Einstein of India.

In **78 CE**, the <u>**Saka era**</u> was founded by Kanishka.

They issued **gold standard coins (22 or 23 carats).**

Ruling over the regions of the <u>**Silk route**</u>, Kushanas greatly benefitted from it. Greater use of saddles in horse riding, armor, turbans, trousers, helmets, long coats and better cavalry are Kushina's contributions.

Scholars in his court: Parsva, Ashvaghosha, Vasumitra, Nagarjuna, Charaka and Mathara.

<u>**Introduced Satrap system:**</u> The Empire was divided into Satrapies under the Satrap. It was during this time that Buddhism began to spread to Korea and Japan also.

<u>**Three distinct schools of art flourished:**</u> Gandhara School in northwest India, Amaravati School in Andhra and the Mathura School in the Ganges valley.

Gandhar   **Mathura**   **Amravati**

It is said that the Kushana period in Indian history was the <u>**predecessor to the golden age of the Gupta period.**</u>

Sanskrit literature began to be developed during this time. The **fourth Buddhist council** was held in <u>**Sanskrit**</u>.

2.8: Gupta Period

Gupta Empire (319-540 AD)

Chandragupta I (319-334 AD)
Samudragupta (335-380 AD)
Chandragupta II (380-414 AD)
Kumargupta I (415-455 AD)
Skandagupta (455-467 AD)

After the fall of the Maurya empire, the **Kushans** in the **North** and the **Satvahanas in the Deccan emerged** as the two major political powers. Guptas are **believed to be feudatories** of the **Kushans**. They are most likely **Vaishyas** in origin. They ruled over **fertile parts** of the **Madhyadesha:** Anuganga (middle Gangetic basin), Saketa (modern Ayodhya, Uttar Pradesh), and Magadha (Bihar).

Probably an important center of power: Prayag (modern Allahabad, Uttar Pradesh) was probably their important center of power. Prayag Prashasti inscription of Samudragupta also supports this opinion.

Probable state seal: **'Garuda'.**

According to the epigraphic evidence, the founder of the dynasty was a person named **"Gupta".**

It is regarded as the Classical Age or Golden Age of Ancient India: all round progress in spheres of art, architecture, Sanskrit literature, stone sculpture, science and technology, metallurgy, and philosophy.

Development of North India: Stable polity, profitable trade, secured and peaceful social set up.

Founder of Gupta Dynasty: **Maharaja Gupta/Sri**

Gupta was the first ruler of the dynasty followed by his son Ghatotkachchh. These two were called Maharajas.

SOURCES OF INFORMATION

➤ **Literacy Sources**

Puranas: Vishnu, Vayu, Bhagvata, Matysa (oldest source) etc.

Kamandaka Nitisara written by Shikhara, prime minister of Chandragupta II.

➢ Kavya-Nataka Literature

- Vishakhadatta: Devi Chandraguptam and Mudrarakshasa.
- Shudraka: Marikchhaktikam.
- Kalidas: Play Vikramourvashiya.
- Pravarsena: Setubandha kavya.
- Vishnu Sharma: Panchatantra.
- Travel account of Fa-Hein.

➢ Inscriptions

Mehrauli Iron Pillar Inscription: refers to the achievements of Chandragupta I.

Allahabad Pillar inscription: important source for the reign of Samudragupta.

Udayagiri Cave Inscription.

Mathura stone Inscriptions.

Sanchi Stone Inscriptions.

Bhitari pillar inscription dates to his reign gives the chronology of Guptas and his conflict with Pushyamitra and Huns.

➢ Seals

- Seal of Dhruvaswamini, queen of Chandragupta II.
- Seal of other officials.
- Vishnu temple at Tigawa.
- Shiva Temple at Bhumara.
- Parvati Temple at Nachana-Kuthara.
- Buddhist shrines at Sanchi and Bodhgaya.
- Dasavatara Temple at Deogarh, etc.

➢ Coins

Every ruler minted their own coins based on their own preferences.
For example, Tiger type, Lyrist type, Ashvamedha type, Archer type, Chhatra type, Lion-slayer type.

Chandragupta-I (319-334AD)

First important ruler was considered the **actual founder** of the dynasty. **Chandragupta I was the first** to be called **Maharajadhiraja (the great king of kings).**

Married to a Lichchhavi princess **Kumaradevi** - expanded it through matrimonial alliance.

His reign covered regions of South Bihar, Jharkhand and parts of Eastern Uttar Pradesh (Saketa and Prayaga).

His accession in about **AD 319-20** marks the beginning of the **Gupta Samvat (era).**

First in Guptas who issued **gold coins (Dinaras)**- bearing the figures of Kumardevi and Chandragupta.

Mehrauli Iron Pillar inscription mentions his extensive conquests.

Samudragupta (335-380 AD)

The son of Chandragupta-I, Samudragupta, became the next ruler whose conquests are recorded in **Prayaga Prashasti (Eulogy)**.

Ardent follower of **Vaishnavism**. Was the **patron of the great Buddhist scholar** Vasubandhu.

Prayaga Prashasti/Allahabad pillar inscriptions:

➢ It was composed by Samudragupta's court poet, a scholar and minister, Harisena in classical Sanskrit and provides a detailed account of his reign

➢ According to Prayaga Prashasti, **Samuddragupta** conquered **Eight kings of Aryavarta.**

➢ The **Allahabad Pillar inscription** mentions that **Samudragupta defeated 12 rulers** in his **South Indian** Expedition (Dakshinapatha).

Samudragupta's policy in South India was different. He did not destroy and annex those kingdoms. **Samudragupta** performed the **Ashwamedh Yajna (sacrifice)** after these achievements.

He issued gold and silver coins - Ashwamedh coins - with the legend Restorer of the Asvamedha.

Kaviraja: Samudragupta was not only a conqueror but also a great poet, musician and patron of learning.

He is called **Napoleon of India** by historian **Vincent Smith.** Allahabad pillar inscriptions called him Dharma Prachar Bandhu. Gave permission to the king of Sri Lanka, Meghavarna to build a monastery in Bodh Gaya.

Chandragupta II (380-414 AD)

Coming to the throne, **Chandragupta-II** defeated the Sakas in western region (Gujarat, Kathiawar and west Malwa), assumed the title of **Sakari** (destroyer of Sakas), **Vikramaditya and ruled from Ujjain.**

Watermark period of Gupta dynasty.

Udayagiri Cave Inscription (Vidisha, MP) and Sanchi inscription give information about this.

He established matrimonial alliances with the Nagas and the Vakatakas. Assumed the title of Parama Bhagavata.

Chandragupta-II was the **first Gupta ruler** to issue **silver coins** bearing lion figures similar in pattern with Saka coins.

Mehrauli iron pillar inscription (Delhi's Qutub-minar complex): records that Chandragupta-II defeated Valikas of Bactria crossing the Sapta Sindhu.

His court had nine jewels or Navaratnas: Kalidasa, Amarsinha, Dhanvantari, Varahmihira, Araruchi, Ghatakarna, Kshapranak, Velabhatt, Shanku.

Chinese Buddhist monk **Fa-Hien** visited his court:

- He visited Peshawar, Mathura, Kanauj, Sravasti, Kapilavastu, Kusinagara, Pataliputra, Kasi and Bodh Gaya among other places.
- He refers to the Gangetic valley as the land of Brahmanism.
- Gives information on the religious, social and economic condition of the Gupta empire.
- He did not mention the name of Chandragupta II.

Kumargupta I (415-455 AD)

Karamdanda (Fyzabad) inscription refers to king **Kumaragupta I as ruler of 4 oceans**, **Mandsor inscription** as ruler of all earth and copper plate inscription of Damodarpur as **Maharajadhiraj**.

Bilsad (Etah) inscription also mentions Kumaragupta I.

Kumaragupta I performed Ashwamedha yajna and assumed titles like Ashwamedha-Mahendra and Mahendraditya. He was also called Shakraditya.

Kumaragupta I was the founder of **Nalanda** University.

Himself a **devotee of Shiva**, Kumaragupta I issued **Kartikeya type coins** bearing the figure of **peacock**.

Skandagupta (455-467 AD)

Son of Kumaragupta I, Skandgupta, during his lifetime bravely fought and **defeated Hunas** on the **North-Western frontier.**

His conquest over **Pushyamitra** is marked in Bhitari Pillar inscription.

Got the **Sudarshan Lake repaired** (Junagadh inscription).

The Gupta Empire declined after the death of Skandagupta in 467 AD.

Vishnugupta (540 CE- 550 CE) was the last recognized Gupta ruler.

SOCIO-ECONOMIC SURVEY OF GUPTA PERIOD

➤ Administration

Gupta kings assumed titles: Paramabhattaraka, Maharajadhiraja, Parameswara, Samrat and Chakravartin.

The most important officers under the Guptas were called the **Kumaramatyas,** with an office of their own called the **Adhikarana.**

<u>**Bhukti**</u> (province) and <u>**Vishaya**</u> (province division) were administrative units headed by **Uparika** and **Vishayapati** respectively.

The king was assisted in his administration by a council consisting of a chief minister, a **Senapati** or commander- in-chief of the army and other important officials. Bureaucracy was not elaborated as that of Maurya.

<u>**Fa-Hien's account**</u> on the <u>**Gupta administration:**</u>

- There was no state interference in the individual's life.
- The administration was so efficient that the roads were kept safe for travelers, and there was no fear of thieves.
- No restrictions on people's movements
- Crimes were negligible.

Important Offices

Mahananda Nayaka- Justice Delivery.

Mahapratisara-Chief of the Guards.

Gramadhyaksha/ gramika - Village headman.

Dutakas- Associated with Gifts and Grants.

Sandhi-Vigrahika- Minister of Peace and War.

Pilupati-Headed Elephants.

Asvapati -Headed Horses.

Nagara Sreshtis- officers looking after the city administration.

Narapati-Headed Foot Soldiers.

Ranabhandagrika- In charge of stores.

Akshapataladhikrita- Superintendent of Records and Accounts.

➤ Economy

Agriculture, trade, commerce and art and crafts all flourished under Guptas.

The King's administration facilitated irrigation, ensured measurement and categorization of land into cultivated **(Kshetra)** and uncultivated **(Khila/ Aprahata)** lands.

The Landowner class (Mahattars, Gramika and Kutumbika) became influential as land was a prestigious property to be sold or gifted.

There was an Increase in land taxes but a decrease in trade and commerce taxes.

Kulyavapa and Dronavapa: terms related to measurement of land.

The king collected taxes varying from one-fourth to one-sixth of the produce.

Two new agricultural taxes: Uparikara (probably a tax imposed on temporary tenants) and Udranga (its exact nature is not clear, but might be water tax or a sort of police tax).

It is confirmed by a general **scarcity of gold coins** after the Guptas. Issued **<u>less pure gold coins than Kushana.</u>**

The Gupta and post-Gupta period witnessed a comparative decline in the country's trade and commerce. The disruption of the north-western trade route by the Huns.

Shreni continued to govern the trader's affairs.

➢ Society and Religion

Society became clearly feudalistic, Brahmins (Brahmadiyas & Agraharas) and feudal chiefs received land grants.

Bhanugupta's Airana (Eran) inscription gives the first evidence of Sati, Child marriage too existed.

Chandalas were the outcaste i.e., out of the 4-fold varna system and made to reside outside village settlements.

Vaishnavite or Shaivite Kings got temples constructed for their respective deities.

Bhagavatism was also identified with Vaishnavism.

Sanskrit was firmly established as the language of royal inscriptions

Idol worship became a common feature.

Gupta kings proclaimed themselves as Bhagavatas (worshippers of Lord Krishna) and Garuda was their emblem.

Religious texts like Puranas, Mahabharata and Ramayana were expanded in this period.

Absorption of tribal communities into Brahminical society.

Assimilation of a large number of foreigners.

Practice of untouchability intensified.

Socio-economic status of shudras improved during this period.

Status of women deteriorated further in the Gupta period. Women lacked property rights. They had full right to their Stridhana. There was no purdah system in the society.

Dharamshastra (law books) texts belonging to the period reflect a tendency towards lowering the age of marriage for girls and advocating a celibate and austere life for widows.

Narada Smriti mentions fifteen types of slaves.

Vishti was forced labour to serve the royal army & officials.

➤ Art and Culture

Continued growth of the Ajanta School (Theme: Buddha's life) was accompanied by the emergence of Bagh School (Hoshangabad in Madhya Pradesh). In this cave-walls were decorated (painted) in local themes.

Ajanta frescoes depict religious scenes of Yakshas, Gandharvas, Apasaras. Sculpture making made considerable growth with evidence of various stone images.

Metal and stone images of Buddha, Shiva and Vishnu are reported from a number of places.

Images of God appeared for the first time.

Stupa and cave construction reduced and temple construction (Nagara styled) picked up:

- Dashavatar Temple, Jhansi, U.P.
- Bhitargaon Temple (Brick) Kanpur, U.P.
- Parvati Temple, Nachnakuthara, M.P.
- Vishnu Temple, Jabalpur, M.P.
- Bagh cave Paintings.

➤ Literature

The Gupta period is considered as the Golden Age of art and literature in ancient India.

Development of literature in Gupta period was diverse as it covered from poetry and play, art (dance and music), philosophy, religion to science, mathematics, physiology, astronomy etc.

There were **Navaratnas, or Nine Gems** in the court of **Chandragupta II** who were experts of particular fields.

Dharmashastras, Narad Smriti, Vishnu Smriti, Brihaspati Smriti and portions of Ramayana and Mahabharata, Bhasa's 12 plays were also written in this period.

Most of the literature is developed using ornate Sanskrit language.

➤ **Science**

Aryabhata: a great mathematician and astronomer, wrote the book Aryabhatiya in 499 CE. It deals with mathematics and astronomy. He was the first to declare that the earth was spherical in shape.

Varahamihira: composed Pancha Siddhantika, the five astronomical systems.

Brihadsamhita is a great work by him in Sanskrit literature which deals with a variety of subjects like astronomy, astrology, geography, architecture, weather, animals, marriage and omens. His Brihadjataka is a standard work on astrology.

Vagbhata: A disciple of Charaka and distinguished physician of Ayurvedic system of medicine from c. 600 CE. He wrote the Ashtanga Hridaya ('Heart of Medicine') and the Ashtangasamgraha ('Tome on Medicine').

Maharishi Palakapya: He wrote the Hastayurveda, a treatise dealing with the diagnosis and treatment of the major diseases of elephants through medication and surgery.

Bhaskara II: Author of the Lilavati written in the 12th century, which contains important ideas of calculus.

Mahavira: A famous 9th century mathematician of Karnataka who lived in the court of the Rashtrakuta king Amoghvarsha, and wrote a book called the Ganitasara Sangraha, which deals with various mathematical problems.

Dhanvantri: He was famous for his knowledge of Ayurveda.

Kashyapa: A 7th century physician who compiled his Ayurvedic knowledge in a compendium which dealt with the diseases of women and children.

Sushruta: The famous author of the Sushruta Samhita, which deals with surgery.

Metallurgy also saw technological advancement in Gupta times. The bronze images of Buddha produced on a considerable scale

The **iron pillar at Mehrauli, Delhi,** standing in the open, which has surprisingly not gathered rust even after fifteen centuries.

DECLINE OF THE GUPTAS

Hun Invasions: Weak successors of Skandagupta could not check growing Hun power and the Hun chief Toramana was able to conquer large parts of western India, stretching up to Eran near Bhopal in central India.

Rise of Feudatories: The Guptas' power was severely curbed by the rise of feudatories. Yashodharman of Malwa, who belonged to the Aulikara feudatory family, successfully challenged the authority of the Guptas.

Gradual Decline in Economic Prosperity: Indicated by the gold coins of later Gupta rulers, which have less gold content and more of alloy. A gradual disappearance of coins in the post-Gupta period is also observed. It led the kings to make payments in the form of land rather than cash. Due to the loss of western India, the rich revenues from foreign trade and commerce also dropped and this further crippled the Guptas.

2.9: Harshavardhana Period (606-647 AD)

Decline of the Gupta Empire was followed by a period of political disorder and disunity in North India. **Harshavardhana's reign** was established in the beginning of the **7th century CE.**

SOURCES OF INFORMATION

Harshacharita written by **Bana** (court poet of Harsha).

Travel accounts of Hiuen Tsang: Chinese traveler who visited India in the 7th century CE.

Dramas written by Harsha - Ratnavali, Nagananda and Priyadarshika.

Inscriptions: Madhuben plate inscription and the Sonpat inscription are helpful to know the ecology of Harsha. Banskhera inscription contains the signature of Harsha.

HARSHAVARDHAN (606–647 CE)

Both **Bana and Hiuen Tsang** portray social life in the times of Harsha. **Pushyabhutis** were **feudatories of Gupta.** They called themselves **Vardhanas.**

<u>Important rulers of this dynasty:</u> Prabhakar vardhana, Adityavardhan and Harshavardhana.

Harshvardhan was son of Prabhakarvardhana.

The Reign of Harsha

Harsha's reign marked the beginning of feudalism in India.

Harshavardhana belonged to the Pushyabhuti Dynasty also called Vardhana Dynasty.

He was a Hindu who later embraced Mahayana Buddhism.

Harshavardhana attacked Shashank of Gauda Kingdom and established his control over regions of Bengal, Bihar and Odisha and befriended Bhashkarvarman of Kamrup (Assam).

Vallabhi King Dhruvbhata in Gujrat too was defeated and a truce was negotiated with him by marriage of Harsha's daughter to Dhruvbhata.

He moved his capital to **Kannauj**.

He assumed titles of Uttarapathanatha or Uttarapathapati (Lord of the North).

While marching southwards, Harshavardhan conquered regions of Malwa and **after crossing Narmada**, he was **<u>defeated by Pulkeshin II</u>** in the Battle of Narmada.

Harshavardhana was greatly influenced by the personality of Hieun Tsang and organized a Buddhist assembly at Kannauj under his chairmanship.

Hieun Tsang, in his book, has appreciated Harshvardhan's justice and munificence (generosity).

Harshavardhan, the able military commander and good administrator, died in 647 CE without heir and is regarded as the last Hindu King to have ruled a large part of North India.

Hence, his death marks the end of Pushyabhuti dynasty and beginning of Muslim rule over North India.

Harsha's Military Conquests

<u>First expedition:</u> Harsha drove out Sasanka from Kannauj. He made Kanauj his new capital. This made him the most powerful ruler of north India.

Harsha fought against **<u>Dhuruvasena II of Valabhi</u>** and defeated him.

Accounts of Hiuen Tsang and the inscriptions of Pulakesin II provide the details of the campaign against **Western Chalukya** ruler Pulakesin II.

Aihole inscription of Pulakesin II mentions the defeat of Harsha by Pulakesin, who after this achievement assumed the title Paramesvara. Hiuen Tsang's accounts also confirm the victory of Pulakesin.

Nepal had accepted Harsha's overlordship.

Harsha established his control over Kashmir and its ruler sent tributes to him.

He also maintained cordial relations with Bhaskaravarman, the ruler of Assam.

Last military campaign: against the kingdom of Kalinga in Orissa and it was a success.

The regions of modern Rajasthan, Punjab, Uttar Pradesh, Bihar and Orissa were under his direct control.

Kashmir, Sindh, Vallabhi and Kamarupa acknowledged his sovereignty.

Harsha and Buddhism

He became an ardent **Hinayana** Buddhist. **Hiuen Tsang converted** him to **Mahayana** Buddhism.

Harsha prohibited the use of animal food in his kingdom.

He erected thousands of monasteries and stupas and established travelers resting places all over his kingdom.

Once in five years he convened a gathering of representatives of all religions.

He brought the Buddhist monks together frequently to discuss and examine the Buddhist doctrine.

➢ Kannauj Assembly

Harsha organized a religious assembly at Kannauj to honor the Chinese pilgrim Hiuen Tsang towards the close of his reign.

He invited representatives of all religious sects. It was attended by scholars from the Nalanda University,

Hinayanists, Mahayanists, Brahmins and Jains.

Hiuen Tsang explained the values of Mahayana doctrine and established its superiority over others.

However, violence broke out and there was also an attempt on the life of Harsha.

> **Allahabad Conference**

Hiuen Tsang mentions the conference held at Allahabad, known as **Prayag.**

It was the one among the conferences routinely convened by Harsha once in five years.

Harsha gave away his enormous wealth as gifts to the members of all religious sects.

SOCIO-ECONOMIC SURVEY OF HARSHAVARDHAN PERIOD

> **Administration**

Harsha governed his empire on the same lines of Gupta.

The basic unit of administration was a village.

Offices under the king became hereditary as **Harisena** who was a 'Mahadandanayaka', or Chief Judicial Officer inherited the office from his father.

One person could bear more than one office as Harisena also held offices of 'Kumaramatya' and 'Sangrahvigrahika'.

Important officers: The 'Sreshti' (Chief Banker or Merchant), the 'Sarthavaha' (Leader of Merchant Caravans), 'Prathama Kulika' (Chief Craftsman), and the 'Kayasthas' (head of the scribes).

Maintenance of public records is an important feature of Harsha rule.

Army: Harsha's army consisted of the traditional four divisions- foot, horse, chariot and elephant. Cavalry and the elephants were much more than that of the Mauryan army.

> **Economy**

Taxes imposed on ports, income from mines and tributes from vassals were other important revenue sources.

One-sixth of the produce was collected as tax and was the main source of revenue.

Overall, trade and commerce are said to have declined during this phase. Rise of self-sufficient economy.

> **Society**

Hiuen-Tsang mentions:

> There were castes, a mix of sub-castes, untouchables and outcastes.

> Forced labor was absent.

> Sudras practiced agriculture.

➤ Three ways of disposal of the dead – cremation, water burial and exposure in the woods.

Fourfold division of society: Brahmins, Kshatriyas, Vaishyas and Shudras

Brahmins were the privileged section of the society and were given land grants by the kings.

Institution of Swayamvara (the ceremony of choosing a husband) had become dysfunctional.

Widow remarriage was not allowed and Sati & dowry systems were prevalent.

➤ Religion

As Harshavardhan was a secular king, all sects of religion peacefully coexisted but Brahmanism grew more than others.

Harshvardhan was a Shiva devotee. Later he converted to Mahayana Buddhism.

According to Hieun Tsang, Harsha held the Allahabad conference once every 5 years.

➤ Art & Culture

A patron of art and literature, Harshavardhan patronized the Banabhatta, Mayura, Matanga Divakara etc.

Banabhatta (biographer of Harsha) wrote Harshacharita, Kadambari & Parvatiparinay.

Harsha was a poet and composed three Sanskrit plays: Nagananda, Ratnavali, and Priyadarshika.

Harshavardhan held 5 yearly donation (Daan) ceremonies at Prayag (Allahabad Conference) and donated money in favor of: Administration, Royal Household, Scholars and Religion.

Brick temple of Laxamana at Sirpur was built during Harsha rule.

Hiuen Tsang describes the glory of the monastery with many storeys built by Harsha at Nalanda.

➤ Nalanda University

The most famous educational institutions were the Hinayana University of Valabhi and the Mahayana University of Nalanda.

The term Nalanda means "giver of knowledge", founded by Kumaragupta I during the Gupta period. Patronized by his successors and later by Harsha.

Renowned professors: Dingnaga, Dharmapala, Sthiramati and Silabadhra.

Dharmapala (native of Kanchipuram) became the head of Nalanda University.

Though it was a Mahayana University, different religious subjects like the Vedas, Hinayana doctrine, Sankhya and Yoga philosophies were also taught. Medium of instruction was **Sanskrit**.

2.10: Sangam Era & South Indian Kingdoms: Pallavas, Chalukyas of Vatapi, Ikshvakus, Kadamba, Kalabhras

South of the Deccan plateau, the land between the Venkatam hills and Kanyakumari is known as the Tamilaham.

The Sangam texts mention three chiefs: Chola, Chera and Pandya.

Sangam Period: Period between the **1st century B.C.** to the end of **2nd century A.D.** in Southern India.

There existed **three Sangams (Academy of Tamil poets)** in ancient Tamil Nadu popularly called **Muchchangam**. These Sangams flourished under the royal patronage of the Pandyas.

2nd and 13th rock edicts of Ashoka named 4 neighborly kingdoms of South India: Cholas, Cheras (Kerala putras of Malabar) Pandyas and Satyaputra.

The Greek authors like Megasthenes, Strabo, Pliny and Ptolemy mention about commercial trade contacts between the West and South India.

The Hathigumpha inscription of Kharavela of Kalinga mentions Tamil kingdoms.

SANGAM LITERATURE

Sangam literature is the main source of History of ancient South India i.e., Tamilkam.

It was compiled during the 3rd century BC to 3rd century CE & was composed in poetic format around themes of love and war.

Sangam was a college or assemblies of Tamil poets held under royal patronage.

Sangam	Venue	Chairman	Remarks
1st	Old Madurai	Agastasya	Attended by Gods & legendary sages. **No Literacy** work of 1st Sangam available.
2nd	Kapadapuram	Agastasya	Only **Tolkappiyam** (grammar book) survives from this.
3rd	New Madurai	Nakkirar	A few of these Tamil literary works have survived and are a useful source to reconstruct the history of Sangam period.

➢ **Sangam Literature is Broadly Divided into 2 Groups**

Narrative texts: called Melkanakku/Eighteen major works consisting of Ettuthogai (Collection of 8 long poems) & Pattupattu (Collection of 10 small poems). Narrative texts are considered heroic poetry in which heroes and wars are glorified. They also give ideas of state formation in South India.

Didactic texts: called Kilkannaku/Eighteen minor works consisting of Tirukural and Naladiyar. These texts prescribe a code of conduct for kings & society.

➢ **Significant Sangam Literature**

Silappadikaram: Written by Ilango Adigal. It is about the love affair of Kovalan, Kanaggi and Madhavi. Later, a Kanaggi Cult developed in South India.

Manimekhalai: Written by Sittalai Sattanar, continues the story of Silappadikaram in the next generation in which Manimekhalai is the daughter of Madhavi and Kovalan.

Tolkappiyam: Written by Tolkappiyar was product of 2nd Sangam and it is basically a work on Tamil grammar & poetics.

Thirukkural: Deals with philosophy and was written by Tiruvallur.

Jeevak Chintamani: Authored by a Madurai-based Jain ascetic Tiruttakkatevar (10th century). The epic is a supernatural fantasy story of a prince who is the perfect master of all arts, perfect warrior, and perfect lover with numerous wives.

Kundalakesi: It appears to be a tragic love story about a Hindu or Jain girl of merchant caste named Kundalakesi who falls in love with Kalan – a Buddhist criminal on a death sentence.

Valayapathi: one of the five great Tamil epics, but one that is almost entirely lost. It is a story of a father who has two wives.

SOUTH INDIAN DYNASTIES

The Sangam literature discusses the **3 main Kingdoms:** Chola, Pandya & Chera and about their rivalry.

➤ CHOLAS

Capitals: **first, at Uraiyur** and later shifted to **Puhar** (Tanjore).

Territory: N-E to the territory of Pandya, between Pennar & Velar Rivers.

Emblem: Tiger.

Centers of trade and industry: Kaverippattanam, Uraiyur and Arikamedu (Puducherry).

Many Sangam Poems mention the Battle of Venni where he defeated the confederacy of Cheras, Pandyas and eleven minor chieftains.

Elara was the earliest known king. He conquered Sri Lanka & ruled over it for 50 years.

Karikala was the greatest king. He founded Puhar & also built irrigation tanks near river Kaveri to provide water for reclaimed land from forest for cultivation.

➤ PANDYAS

Capital: **Madurai** (center of trade and industry).

Territory: Southernmost & South eastern portion of peninsula.

Emblem: Carp (fish).

Pandyas had trade relations with Romans. They were first mentioned by Megasthenes. They also find mention in the Ramayana & Mahabharata.

Nedunjelian, known for his kingdom's wealth and prosperity, was the most noteworthy Pandya ruler.

Maduraikkanji was written by Mangudi Maruthainar which describes the socio-economic condition of the flourishing seaport of Korkai.

➤ CHERAS

Capital: at **Vanji** (Malabar).

Important seaports: Tondi and Musiri.

Territory: West & North of Pandya.

Emblem: Bow and Arrow.

Senguttuvan (Red Chera) was the most important ruler. He established the Kannagi or Pattini Cult; Kannagi became the object of worship.

He was the first King from South India to send an ambassador to China.

His military achievements have been chronicled in epic Silapathikaram.

He enjoyed the reputation of being highly ethical or virtuous.

Gajabahu was his contemporary Sri Lankan King.

Karrur and Mujirispattanam were important centers of international trade.

Romans settled at Muziris Pattanam.

The Temple of Roman emperor Augustus was constructed here.

3. Medieval History

Medieval History is the **Journey** from <u>**Battle of Tarain**</u> to <u>**Battle of Plassey**</u> via **Battle of Panipant.**

3.1: Early Medieval Period

Early Medieval Period is a **transsitional phase** between Ancient and Medieval periods. It was distinguished by the emergence of numerous states at Local levels.

After the **death of Harshavardhana** (in 647 AD), **Lalitaditya (Karkota** Dynasty of Kashmir) briefly controlled Punjab, **Kanauj** and parts of Bengal, but his power diminished with the rise of other kingdoms.

Several large states emerged in the Noth India, Deccan and South India. **However, unlike** the empires of the Guptas and Harsha, these North Indian kingdoms were **unable to exert control** over the entire **Ganga Valley.** There was a **Tripartite Contest** between <u>**Pratiharas**</u> (Jalore, Rajasthan), <u>**Palas**</u> (Bengal) and <u>**Rashtrakutas**</u> (Deccan)

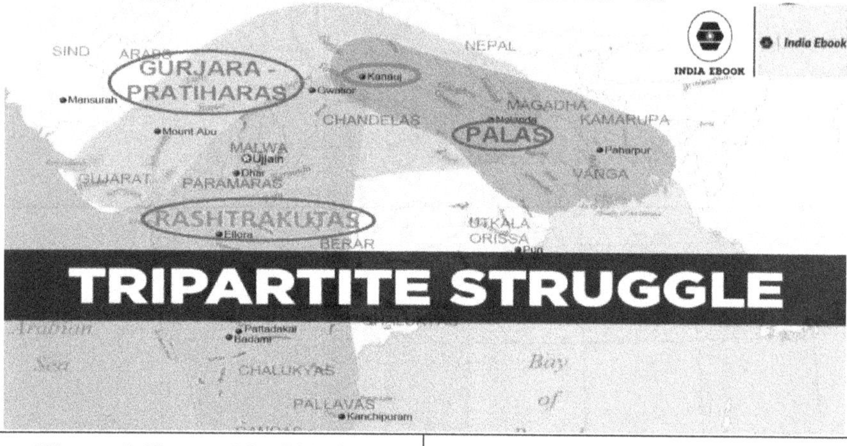

Phase -I (Started in 790 CE)		Phase – II	
Round 1	Dharmapala (Palas) vs. **Vatsaraja (Pratiharas)**	Round 1	Dharmapala (Palas) vs. **Nagabhatta-II (Pratiharas)**
Round 2	**Dhruva (Rashtrakutas)** vs. Vatsaraja (Pratiharas)	Round 2	**Govinda-III** (Rashtrakutas) vs Nagabhatta-II (Pratiharas)
Round 3	Dharmapala (Palas) vs. **Dhruva (Rashtrakutas), In 793 CE** **Dhruva** died. Then Dharmapala placed Chakrayuda at Kanauj		

Final Result: G. Pratiharas ruled the Kanauj.

Tripartite Struggle

➢ The Palas (750–1161 AD)

• The Pala Empire, was founded by **Gopala** (750–770 AD) and known as the "Kingdom of Dharma" by the Arabs. He founded a **Buddhist Mahavihara at Odantapuri (Bihar).**

• **Dharmapala** assumed the titles Paramesvara, Parambhattaraka and Maharajadhiraja. He founded **Vikaramashila monastery** in **Bhagalpur (Bihar).** Khalimpur copper plate inscription mentions the extent of his kingdoms.

• **Devapala** extended Pala control eastwards up to **Kamarupa** (Assam). He defeated the **Rashtrakuta** ruler, **Amoghavarsha.**

• The rise of the **Pratiharas in Jalore** under **Mihira Bhoja** and the advance of the Rashtrakutas into Pala territories inevitably brought about the decline of the Palas.

• They were devout **Buddhists** and promoted **Mahayana Buddhism.**

➢ Gujara Pratiharas (Agnikula Rajputs) (8th–11th Century AD)

• Founded by **Harichandra** and called **Al-Jurz** by Arabs.

• They captured a large part of **Madhyadesh** and **Kanauj** by the **9th century.** Initially ruling from Bhilmal, they subsequently shifted their capital to Kanauj.

• The Pratiharas were noted for their **opposition to Arab forces** and their strategic conflicts with the Palas and the Rashtrakutas.

• Their imp rulers include **Nagabhatta I** (730-760 AD), **Vatsaraja** (780-800 AD), **Nagabhatta II** (800-833 AD) & **Mihir Bhoja** (836-885 AD).

• **Nagabhatta II** revived the dynasty and his suzerainty was recognised by rulers of western Kathiawar, Andhra, Kalinga and Vidarbha.

• **Bhoja** consolidated a vast empire stretching from Punjab and Kathiawar to Koshal and Kanauj, with several contemporary powers acknowledging his suzerainty.

• Subsequent weaker rulers couldn't maintain the vast empire, facing assaults from the Rashtrakutas.

➢ The Rashtrakutas (753-975 AD)

• The Rashtrakutas, referred to as **Ballahara** by the Arabs, emerged as a significant power around 743 AD in the **Deccan**, ruling from their **capital at Manyakheta**, present-day **Malkhed.**

• The important rulers include **Dantivarman or Dantidurga** (735–756 AD), **Dhruv Dharavarsha** (779- 793 AD), **Amoghavarsha I** (814–880 AD), **Krishna III** among others.

• **Dhruv Dharavarsha** (779-793 AD) marked the dynasty's northern expedition, defeating prominent rulers like **Vatsaraja (Pratihara king)** and **Dharmapala (Pala king)**

• **Amoghavarsha I** composed one of the **earliest Kannada literature** texts, the Kavirajamarga. He took the titles Nripatunga, Atishayadhavala, Maharaja-shanda and Vira-Narayana.

○ The decline of the Rashtrakutas began under his reign due to weaker military acumen. Under his successor, Krishna II, the kingdom experienced further decay.

• The three gems of ancient Kannada literature–**Kavichakravarthi Ponna**, **Adikavi Pampa** and **Kavichakravarti Ranna** – were patronised by **Rashtrkuta king Krishna III**, as well as by Tailapa and Satyashraya of Western Chalukyas.

Dynasties of the North (including Rajput Dynasties)

➤ **Chandelles** of Jejakabhukti (Bundelkhand) (9th-13th century AD)

The Chandella dynasty was founded by **Nannuka**.

Important rulers include: Yasovarman, Vidyadhara and Paramardideva.

Architectural legacy is visible in the magnificent **temples at Khajuraho.**

➤ **Paramaras of Malwa (9th-14th century AD)**

• They were originally vassals of the Pratiharas and the Rashtrakutas.

○ **Upendra/Krishnaraja** founded it with **Dhar** as its **capital.**

• Important rulers include: **Munja/ Vakapatiraja II** and **Raja Bhoja.**

• Under **Raja Bhoja**, the dynasty reached its **zenith under his reign.** He authored books on subjects like medicine, astronomy, religion, and architecture. He founded the city of Bhojapur near Bhopal.

• **Mahālakadeva** (died 1305 AD), the last ruler of the Paramara dynasty, was defeated by the forces of Alauddin Khalji.

➤ **Tomaras of Dhillika (Delhi) (8th-12th century AD)**

They ruled the Hariyana (Haryana) with their capital at Dhillika (Delhi) and were the **feudatory of the Pratiharas.**

They often had conflicts with the **Chahamanas of Shakambhari**, and the Chahaman followed their rule.

The most important king was **Anangapala Tomara**. He established Delhi, and he was described in the 11th-century inscription of the Iron pillar at Mehrauli.

Anangapala II was the founder of the **citadel of Lal Kot** in the Mehrauli area and also built a tank known as the **Anang Tal.**

The **Suraj Kund reservoir** (near Faridabad, Haryana) was commissioned by the **Surajpala.**

> **Chahmanas or Chauhans of Sakambhari (6th- 12th century AD)**

• The dynasty was named after their capital, **Sambhar** in Rajasthan. It was founded by **Simharaja**.

• Important rulers include: Ajayaraja (founded Ajmer), Prithviraj III and Vigraharaja IV (Constructed the Adhai din ka Jhonpra (now mosque) which was originally a college).

• **Chandbardai** wrote **Prithviraj Raso** (in Braj Bhasa) on the life of **Prithviraj III**. Prithviraj fought two wars with Muhammad Ghori.

o 1st Battle of Tarain (1191): It ended in victory for the Rajputs.

o 2nd Battle of Tarain (1192): Prithviraj lost to Muhammad Ghori.

> **Gahadvalas of Kannauj (11th-12th century AD)**

They were **Suryavanshi Kshatriyas** who ruled the kingdom of **Kannauj** in the late 11th century.

Important rulers include: Chandradeva (founded this dynasty), Vijayachandra and Jaichandra.

In the **Battle of Chandawar** (1194 AD), Mohammad Ghori defeated Jaichandra and sacked the kingdom.

Jaichandra's grandson, Siyaji, founded the Rathore clan, which ruled the princely state of Marwar from Jodhpur.

> **Kalachuris of Tripuri (10th- 12th century AD)**

• Founded by **Kokalla-I** (845-855 AD). They are also known as Katasuris, Haihayas, and Chedis. Their earliest seat of power was **Mahishmati** on the Narmada.

• The famous poet **Rajasekhara** lived in the **Kalachuri court.**

> **Chalukyas (Solanki) of Gujarat (950-1300 AD)**

Important rulers include: Bhima I, Jayasimha Siddharaja and Kumarpala. During the reign of **Bhima**, Mahmud Ghazni invaded Gujarat and looted the Somnath temple.

During the reign of Kumarapala's minor grandson, Gujarat faced Muhammad Ghur's invasion.

Karna II, the last **Hindu king of Gujarat**, confronted Alauddin Khalji's forces.

➤ Kashmir

• In Kashmir, the <u>Karkota dynasty</u>, known for its rulers like **Lalitaditya and Muktapida,** wassucceeded by the Utpalas in the mid-9th century.

• **Avantivarman** (855-883 AD), the founder of the <u>Utpala dynasty</u>, significantly developed drainage and irrigation systems to provide relief from floods.

• The reign of the renowned **Queen Didda** was marked by unrest and led to the rise of the <u>Lohara dynasty</u>.

Key Dynasties of East and North-East India

➤ Assam

• The **Pralamba dynasty** emerged in the **ninth century** in the Assam region. An **unidentified king** from this dynasty successfully <u>repelled Bakhtiyar Khalji's attack,</u> inflicting significant losses on the invaders.

• By the mid-13th century, the <u>Ahoms</u>, a subgroup of the Shan tribe, established the Ahom Kingdom, leading to the region being named "Assam". The Ahom state depended upon forced labour. Those forced to work for the state were called paiks.

➤ Varmans and Senas of East Bengal (11th Century AD)

The <u>Varmans</u> rose to power in the early 11th century, succeeded by the <u>Senas</u>, who likely originated from the Kannada-speaking region and claimed links with the kings of Dakshinapatha.

Vijayasena reign detailed in the Deopara Prasahsti inscription (stone inscription). His successor, **Ballala Sena**, was noted for his learning, authorship, and the introduction of the social system of Kulinism.

Lakshmanasena, the last Hindu ruler of Bengal and son of Ballal Sena, known for his cultural advancements, had notable literary figures like **Jayadeva (Gita Govinda)**, Halayudha and Sridharadasa at his court.

➤ Kalinga, Orissa

• In the mid-7th century, Orissa was under the rule of Sainyabhita Madhavavarman (Srinivasa) of the Shailodbhava dynasty, noted for performing the Ashwamedha sacrifice.

- The **Eastern Gangas**, related to the Gangas of Mysore, established their domain in Kalinga, with Kalinganagara as their capital.
- Anantavarman Chodaganga laid the foundation for modern Orissa and constructed the Jagannath temple.
- **Narasimha I** (1238-1264 AD) commissioned the construction of Sun Temple at Konark.
- In the mid-15th century, a new royal family, the Suryavamsas, came to power in Kalinga. **Lingaraj temple, Bhubaneswar** (related to Shiva), was built by Somvanshi King Yayati I.

<table><tr><td>Key Dynasties of Deccan and South India</td></tr></table>

➢ Chalukyas of Kalyani (10th-12th century AD)

Taila II (973-997 AD), the founder of **Chalukyas of Kalyani**, succeeded the Rashtrakutas, with their capital established in Kalyani (modern Bidar district), Karnataka.

Vikramaditya VI established the **Chalukya-Vikram era** in place of the Saka era. He was a patron to eminent scholars like Bilhana, the composer of Vikramanankadevacharita, and Vijnaneshvara, the author of Mitakshara.

The period marked a notable **Chalukya-Chola rivalry**, tacitly accepting the Tungabhadra River as the border between the two kingdoms.

➢ Yadavas of Devagiri

- They claimed to have a **lineage** of the **Yadu family** of **Lord Krishna**, and are believed to be an indigenous Maratha group. **Bhillama V** founded the Yadava kingdom with **Devagiri as its capital.**
- The last famous ruler of this dynasty was **Rama Chandra Deva**, who faced invasion by Alauddin Khalji.

➢ Kakatiyas of Warangal (950-1323 AD)

Originating from an ancient Telugu family, they were feudatories to the Western Chalukyas.

Important rulers include: Ganapati, Rudramadevi and Pratap Rudra.

Ganapati, a prominent Kakatiya ruler, centralised power over the Telugu region, emphasizing administrative efficiency and bolstering trade and agriculture.

Motupalli was the chief port of the Kakatiyas and Venetian traveler Marco Polo visited this port.

➤ Cholas of Thanjavur (later half of 9th-13th century AD)

Rajaraja I (985-1014 AD)

- His era has been compared with Samudraguta in its political significance.
- He constructed the Brihadesvara temple at Thanjavur (known as Rajarajeswara temple after him).
- He also assisted the king of Java in constructing a Buddhist Vihara in Java.

Rajendra I (1014-44 AD)

- He assumed the title of Gangaikonda (conqueror of the Ganges) and founded the city of Gangaikonda Cholapuram after his victory over Mahipala (the king of the Pala dynasty).
- The Gangaikonda Cholapuram temple was built to commemorate his victories in North India.
- He adopted the titles of Mudikonda Cholan (the crowned Chola), Kadaramkondan (conqueror of Kadaram), and Pandita Cholan (scholarly Cholan).
- He conquered Sumatra and promoted trade between the Malaya peninsula and South India. His naval operation was directed against Sri Vijaya kingdom (southern Sumatra), a prominent maritime and commercial state.

Kulottunga I (1070-1122 AD)

- He was the last important Chola ruler who united the Eastern Chalukyas of Vengi with the Cholas.
- Initiated administrative reforms, including land surveys.
- Though a Shaivite, he made grants to Buddhist shrines at Nagapattam.

3.2: Advent of Islam in India

Muhammad Bin Qasim eventually established **Arab rule** in **Sind in 712 AD** after **defeating King Dahir**.

Ghaznavids in India

Mahmud Ghazni, invaded India **17 times**. As a reward for his service to Islam, he received the title of **'Yamin al-Dawla'** from the Abbasid Caliph.

- He defeated **Jaipal (Hindushahi ruler)** in **1001 A.D**. He defeated **Anandpal (Jaipal's son)** in the Battle of Waihind (1008-1009 AD).

• He attacked the cities of Nagarkot, Thanesar, Mathura and Kanauj and looted the **Somnath temple in 1025 AD.**

Ghurids in India

Muhammad of Ghor or **Muhammad Ghori's** first invasion was against Multan, which ultimately fell in 1175 AD.

• He was defeated in Gujarat by Raja Bhimdev II (Chalukya/Solanki dynasty) in the Battle of Kayadara in 1178-79, near Mount Abu.

• He fought two battles with Prithviraj

○ First Battle of Tarain (1191): Prithviraj won this battle but failed to consolidate his position.

○ Second battle of Tarain (1192): Prithviraj suffered defeat.

• Battle of Chandawar (1194): Mohammad Ghori defeated **Jai Chand** (Gadhawal king of Kannauj).

3.3: The Delhi Sultanate
Slave or Mamluk Dynasty (1206-1290 AD)

➤ **Qutub-ud-din Aibak (1206-1210 AD)**

Qutub-ud-din Aibak severed relations with Ghazni after Ghori's death and founded the Slave dynasty in India, declaring himself the Sultan, with Lahore as the capital of his kingdom.

He is also known as **"Lakh Baksh"** (Donor of lakhs)

Constructed two mosques: Quwat-ul-Islam in Delhi and Arhai din ka Jhonpra in Ajmer.

Commissioned the construction of **Qutub Minar** dedicated to **Sufi saint Khwaja Qutubuddin Bakthiyar Kaki.**

Tajul-Ma'asir (the first history book of the Delhi Sultanate) was written by Hasan Nizami under his patronage.

➤ **Shams-ud-din Iltutmish (1210-1236 AD)**

• He was the slave and **son-in-law of Qutub-Uddin-Aibak** and succeeded him after defeating his son. So he is also called 'slave of a slave'. He belongs to the **Ilbari tribe.**

• Iltutmish is considered the real consolidator of Turkish conquests in northern India.

• The **first Mongol invasion** of India took place in his reign. But he saved India from Mongols (Genghis Khan) by refraining from supporting

Khwarizm Jalaluddin, a Central Asian ruler, in his battle against the Mongols.

• **Shifted** the <u>**capital from Lahore to Delhi**</u>. Appointed elite military slaves (Bandagan), imported from centres like Bukhara, Samarqand, and Baghdad, as governors and generals.

• He <u>**formed Chahalgani/Chalisa**</u> (council of 40 members) to administer the Sultanate.

• Introduced **copper (Jital)** and **silver coins (tanka)**, the **two basic coins** of the Sultanate period.

• Qutb Minar, a colossal victory tower, completed during his reign.

• Started the **Iqta system** in India.

> #### Razia Sultan (1236-1240 AD)

Only female Muslim ruler of the Sultanate. According to <u>**Ibn Battuta**</u>, she defied norms by riding horses, being armed, discarding the veil system, wearing male attire, and leading the army in war.

Power struggle between the monarchy and the Turkish chiefs (Chahalgani) started during her reign.

The elevation of a slave, Jalal-ud-din Yaqut, to the post of Amir-i-Akhur, Master of the Stables, angered the Turkish nobles. She was later assassinated while suppressing a rebellion in southern Punjab.

> #### Balban (1266-1287 AD)

• He was intolerant of criticism and extremely authoritarian. After consolidating his power, he assumed the <u>**title of Zil-e-Ilahi.**</u>

• He **abolished Chalisa/Chahalgani** because of its growing influence in the administration.

• He enforced ceremonies like **Sijada** (prostration) and **Paiboss** (kissing the monarch's feet)-symbolising that nobles were not his equals.

• Maintained an extensive network of spies in the government departments.

• Balban adopted the policy of **'blood and iron'** to deal with robbers and dacoits on the roads in Awadh and Ganga-Jamuna doab region and suppressing Meos (inhabitants of Mewat region), who plundered the outskirts of Delhi. Military outposts (thanas) were set up around Delhi.

• Balban reorganised the **military department (Diwan-i-Arz)** and provided pensions to soldiers no longer fit for service.

Khilji Dynasty (1290 - 1320 AD)

➢ Jalaluddin Khilji (1290-1296 AD)

He did not exclude the Turks from high offices but ended their monopoly of high offices.

He **moderated Balban's strict policies**, asserting that with a Hindu majority, the state couldn't be solely Islamic, thus, **displaying a tolerant approach towards Hindus.**

He was killed by his nephew and son-in-law, Alauddin Khalji, who subsequently ascended the throne.

➢ Alauddin Khilji (1296-1316 AD)

• He took the **title** of <u>Sikander-i-Azam.</u>

• He introduced the **Chehra** (description of soldiers) and **Dagh** (branding of horse) system.

• He was the **first Sultan** to pay soldiers in **cash instead of shares of booty** and had the largest standing army of all the Delhi rulers.

• He defended against the **Mongol invasion** led by **Targhi** who marched up to Delhi and besieged the city.

Administration

• Centralised revenue collection directly from the farmers. Tax policies primarily targeted the wealthy rather than burdening the poor.

• Traditional village officials, **khots** (smaller landlords) and **muqaddams** (village headmen) were stripped of their customary privileges. He taxed them at the same rate as peasants and subjected them to **Charai** (grazing tax) and **Ghari taxes** (House tax).

• He established a postal system to maintain communication across the empire.

• He established a **spy service** to monitor the activities and discussions of nobles.

• He famously proclaimed **'Kingship knows no kinship'**.

• **Banned** wines and intoxicants; Gambling was forbidden.

• He stored grains in **royal granaries to mitigate famines** and control prices.

• To sustain a large army on modest pay, he ensured **low prices for essential commodities** by setting maximum prices for items including grains, cloth, fruits, livestock, and even slaves and horses.

- **Price control** was done through an extensive intelligence network to keep an eye on black-marketing and hoarding.
- The **sera-i-adl** for cloth, sugar, herbs, dry fruits, butter, and lamp oil; another for horses, slaves, and cattle.
- **Kharaj** - agriculture tax amounting to about 50 per cent of the peasant's produce. For collecting kharaj, a particular post of the officer was created known as Mustakharaj.
- **Biswa** (1/20 of bigha) was used for cultivable land measurement and calculating its productivity.
- The land tax generally had to be paid in cash, pushing peasants into the money market. While in the **Doab region**, the tax was collected on grain for future scarcity.

<u>**Art and Architecture**</u>

- **He supported poets of his period: Amir Khusrau and Mir Hasan Dehlvi.**
- o Honored Amir Khusrau with the title of **Tuti-i-Hind** (Parrot of India).
- o **<u>Khazain-ul-Futuh</u>** by **Amir Khusrau** describes the conquests undertaken by Alauddin.
- **Architecture: He constructed:**
- o **<u>Alai Darwaza (1311):</u>** the southern gateway of the Quwwat-ul-Islam Mosque in Qutb complex, Mehrauli, Delhi.
- o **<u>Siri Fort (1303):</u>** Situated north of the Qutub complex.
- o **<u>Mosque Jamait Khanm:</u>** Built within the enclosure of Nizam-ud-din Aulia's shrine.

Tughlaq Dynasty (1320 AD TO 1413 AD)

➤ Ghiyasuddin Tughlaq (1320-1325 AD)	GST

- He belonged to the Qarauna tribe of Turks and was the founder of the Tughlaq dynasty.
- He was the <u>**first Sultan to construct canals.**</u>
- Tughlakabad Fort was built by Ghiyasudddin Tughlaq (1321) in Delhi.
- **Amir Khusrau's "Tughlaq Nama"** is a biography of Ghiyasuddin along with other Tughlaq rulers.

➤ Mohammad Bin Tughlaq (1325-1351 AD)	MBT

His reign marked both the zenith and the onset of decline for the Delhi Sultanate. Moroccan traveller Ibn-Batuta served as his envoy to China.

He established the **Diwan-i-Amir-Kohi**, a separate department promoting agriculture by providing loans (known as 'Taccavi loans') to induce them to cultivate superior crops.

First Sultan to have participated in the **festival of Holi.**

Enhanced taxation and cesses in 1336 in the Ganga-Yamuna doab region.

He **first shifted** the <u>**capital from Delhi to Devagiri (Daulatadab)**</u> for improved control over south India but the transfer proved disastrous.

He launched a **token currency**, with bronze coins equated to silver tanka coins value..

Proposed Khurasan Expedition (1329) to conquer Khurasan and Iraq, which was later abandoned.

He died in 1351 when he was marching towards Sindh on which Badauni commented "The king was freed from his people and they from their King."

> ### Firoz Shah Tughlaq (1351-1388 AD)   FST

Soldiers were not paid in cash but by assignments of the land revenue of villages.

Established <u>**Wakil-i-Dar**</u> - Responsible for court decorum and noble precedence.

Created a **public works department** responsible for construction in the towns of Fatehabad, Hissar, Firozpur, Jaunpur, and Firuzabad

Two pillars of Ashoka were brought to Delhi, one from Meerut and the other from Topara.

Amassed a huge number of slaves and established a department for slaves **(Diwan-i-Bandagan).**

He established <u>hospitals</u> for the poor known as **"Dar-ul-shafa".**

Diwan-i-Khairat for providing for the <u>**marriages of poor girls.**</u>

He introduced two new coins: The **Adha** (equivalent to 50% of a Jital) and the **Bikh** (equivalent to 25% of a Jital).

<u>**Jizyah**</u> was imposed as **a separate tax** by **Firoz Shah Tughlaq** which was previously collected in conjunction with land revenue.

He imposed four taxes sanctioned by Islamic law: **Kharaj** (land tax); **Khams** (1/5 of the looted property during wars); **Jizya** (religious tax on

Hindus); **Zakat** (2½ per cent of the income of Muslims, used for the welfare of Muslim subjects and their religion).

He became the **first Sultan to impose a Sharb** (irrigation tax).

He wrote his autobiography titled 'Fatuhat-i-Firozshahi'(Persian).

Zia-ud-Din Barani wrote 'Fatawa-i-Jahandari' and 'Tarikh-i-Firozshahi'.

Firuz Tughlaq was the first ruler who initiated the translation of Hindu religious works from Sanskrit into Persian.

He founded the city of Jaunpur in memory of his cousin Mohammed bin Tughlaq. He also built the Kotla Fort in Delhi.

Sayyid Dynasty (1414 -1451 AD)

• After Firoz Shah Tughlaq, the rulers were weak. Timur's (Mongol chieftain) invasion in 1398 plundered northern India. While leaving India, he appointed Khizar Khan as the governor of Multan, Lahore, and Dipalpur.

• **<u>Khizr Khan</u>** (1414-1421 AD) took over Delhi and started the **Sayyid dynasty.**

• His reign and that of his successors were marked by efforts to quell rebellions in regions like Kateher, Badaun, Etawah, and others, as well as contending with the Sharqi sultans of Jaunpur.

• After he died in 1421, he was succeeded by Mubarak Shah (1421-1433 CE), Muhammad Shah (1434-1443 CE), and Alauddin Alam Shah (1445-1451), who were not very influential leaders.

• The sayyids put on a pointed **cap (kulah)** and were known as **'Kulah-Daran'.**

Lodi Dynasty (1451-1526 AD)

➤ **Bahlul Lodi (1451-1489 AD)**

He founded the Lodhi dynasty and succeeded in bringing a large area of North India under his control. He annexed the Jaunpur kingdom.

He was given the title Khan-i-khanan after successfully helping Muhammad Shah against the Malwa Sultan.

➤ **Sikandar Lodi (1489-1517 AD)**

• He was the son of Bahlul Lodi. The Lodi Empire in North India attained its zenith under him.

• He was contemporary of both Mehmud Begarha of Gujarat and Rana Sanga of Mewar.

- He abolished the 'zakat' tax on grains.
- Introduced a new unit of measurement called the Gaz-i-Sikandari.
- Reimposed the Jaziya tax on non-muslims.
- Established the city of Agra and relocated the capital from Delhi to Agra in 1506.
- He was a well-known poet and wrote with the pen name Gulrukhi.

➢ Ibrahim Lodi (1517-1526 AD)

He served as the last Sultan of the Lodi Dynasty in Delhi.

- Succession dispute led to the division of the empire. This weakened the central power and led to internal conflict.
- Daulat Khan Lodhi, the governor of Punjab, invited Babur to overthrow Ibrahim Lodhi. Babur accepted the offer and defeated Ibrahim in the First Battle of Panipat (1526). Thus ending the Delhi Sultanate.

Key Aspects of Delhi Sultanate Administration

➢ Iqta System

- Iqta is an Arabic word and the institution started in Persia (Iran). It Used in the Caliphate administration as a way of financing operations and paying civil and military officers.
- The rulers made revenue assignments (Iqta), instead of cash to their nobles (umara).
  - o The assignees (known as muqti and wali) collected revenue from these areas.
  - o The collected revenue was for their expenses, paying the troops (maintained by them), and sent the surplus (fawazil) to the centre.
- It was non-hereditary and did not imply a right to the land, but it became hereditary under Firuz Shah Tughlaq. These revenue assignments were transferable, with the iqta-holder being transferred from one region to another every three or four years.

➢ Important Offices

__Naib or Wali:__ Most influential position and oversaw all departments with extended authority.

__Diwan-i-wazirat:__ Led the finance department.

__Diwan-i-Ariz:__ Defense minister, overseeing military affairs with the Ariz-i-mumalik heading thedepartment, responsible for soldier recruitment.

Diwan-i-Risalat: Headed by the chief Sadr; the Department managed religious matters.

Qazi: Chief Qazi headed the judicial department overseeing Sharia in civil cases.

Diwan-i-Insha: Managed correspondence, handling all communications between the ruler and officials.

Wakil-i-Dar: Maintaining the decorum of the court.

Barids: Intelligence agents

Karkhanas: They served the Sultan's needs, producing luxurious items like silk, gold, silver etc.

➢ Local Administration in Delhi Sultanate

AREA	GOVERNED BY
Iqtas (Province)	Muqtis (Governor)
Ships (Districts)	Shiqdar
Pargana (Blocks)	Amil (Revenue Collector)
Village (Basit unit of Administration)	Muqaddam or Chaudhari

➢ Land Categorization

Iqta land: Lands that officials received as iqtas in lieu of payment for their services.

Khalisa land: Directly controlled by the Sultan, revenues designated for the royal court and royal household expenses.

Inam land: Land granted to religious leaders or institutions.

➢ Agriculture

• Food crops, cash crops, fruits, vegetables, and spices were cultivated (account of Ibn Battutah), including sericulture, using techniques like crop rotation, double cropping, three-crop harvesting, and fruit grafting.

• Artificial water-lifting devices like the Persian wheel were used.

➢ Amir Khusrau

• Innovated musical instruments like the tabla and sitar.

• Also known as the **"Parrot of India" or "Tuti-i-hind"**.

• Played a pivotal role in creating new ragas and qawwalis.

• He also compiled **"Tughlaq Nama"** and lauded Kashmir as a paradise on earth.

3.4: Vijaynagar Empire

After asserting their **independence from Hoysala rulers** (after the death of **Ballal III**), **Harihara and Bukka** laid the foundation of the Vijayanagara Empire in **1336**.

Vidyaranya, a respected Saiva saint and Sanskrit scholar, is believed to have played a pivotal role in founding the Empire.

Initially, the **capital** was near **Anegondi** (north bank of Tungabhadra), **later shifted to Hoysala town, Hosapattana** (near Hampi; south bank of Tungbhadra), and renamed Vijayanagara (city of victory). **Hampi** derived its name from the **local mother goddess, Pampadevi**.

Four dynasties governed the Vijayanagar kingdom for **over three centuries:**

DYNASTY	FOUNDER	TIMELINE
Sangama	Harihara I	1336-1485
Saluva	Saluva Narsimha	1485-1505
Tuluva	Viranarsimha	1505-1570
Aravidu	Tirumala	1570-1650

➢ **Sangama Dynasty**

Harihara (1336-56 AD)

• Defeated the **Hoysala ruler of Mysore** and executed him. His brother, Bukka succeeded him.

• He founded a **new city** on the South bank of a tributary to river Krishna and undertook to rule his **new kingdom** as the agent of a deity to whom all the land south of the river Krishna was supposed to belong.

Deva Raya I (1404-1422 AD)

• He was defeated by the **Bahmani ruler Firuz Shah**. Later, he entered into an **alliance** with **Warangal**, which changed the balance of power in the Deccan and defeated Firuz Shah Bahmani and annexed the entire Reddi territory up to the mouth of Krishna River.

• He constructed **a dam across** the **Tungabhadra** and **Hiradra** rivers and used canals to counter the shortage of water.

• **Nicolo Conti** visited Vijaynagar in 1420.

Devaraya II (1422–46 AD)

• Greatest ruler of the **Sangama dynasty**. He defeated the Gajapati rulers of Odisha.

• According to Ferishta (Court Historian of Deccan Sultans), he recruited trained Muslim cavalry and gave archery training to his soldiers.
• **Abdur Razaak** visited **Zamorin** of Kochi and the Vijayanagar court during his reign.
• According to **Nuniz**, the kings of Sri Lanka and Tennasserim (Malay and Burma) paid tribute to him.

➤ **Tuluva Dynasty**

Krishna Deva Raya (1509–29 AD)

He was also known as Andhra Bhoj.

Fought battle on two fronts: Bahmani Sultans (traditional enemy) and the Gajapati rulers of Orissa.

Acquired the **Raichur Doab** (1512), subdued rulers of **Orissa (1514)**, and defeated the **Sultan of Bijapur (1520)**.

Founded a **suburban township** near Vijayanagar called **Nagalapuram**, named after his mother.

He added gopurams to some important temples like Vijay Mahal and Vittala Swamy Temple.

Foreign visitors **Domingo Paes**, **Fernao Nuniz** and **Duarte Barbosa** praised Krishnadevaraya's character and the opulence of Vijayanagara City.

He was a gifted scholar of **Telugu and Sanskrit**. His works include:

○ Renowned Telugu poem **Amuktamalyada** (the story of Andal and a treatise stating the instance of Lord Vishnu in his dream).

○ Madalasa Charita, Satyavedu Parinaya, Rasamanjari, Jambavati Kalyanam (Sanskrit),

○ Krishna Deva Rayana Dinachari (Kannada)

He **patronised Ashtadiggajas**, the **eight** celebrated **poets of Telugu.**

○ Allasani Peddana (also known as Andhrakavita Pitamaga), his works include: Manucharitam and Harikathasaram;

○ Tenali Ramakrishna (Court jester and poet): work includes Panduranga Mahatyam.

The taxation system of Krishna Deva:

(1) The tax rate on land was fixed depending on the quality of the land.

(2) Private owners of workshops paid an industry tax.

➢ Sadasiva Raya (1543-67 AD)

• Real power laid in the hands of his minister Rama Raya, who got support from kinsmen (of Aravidu clan) by appointing them as Nayak of strategic localities.

• Rama Raya was a great warrior and strategist. He fought with the Bijapur ruler. However, later, he allied with Bijapur against Golkonda and Ahmadnagar, all of which eventually led to the Battle of Talikota.

➢ Battle of Talikota (1565 AD)

• The battle was fought at Talikota or Rakshasi-Tangadi in 1565 between Vijayanagar and Deccan states (combined armies of Bijapur, Ahmadnagar, and Golconda).

• Rama Raya personally commanded the forces; however, he lost the battle and was later executed.

• The victorious Bahmani armies entered Vijayanagar city for the first time in history and ransacked it for several months. This battle is generally considered the signal for the end of Vijayanagar.

➢ Administration (Vijayanagar Empire)

• The king was the ultimate authority and was assisted by several high-ranking officers.

o Mahapradhani (Chief minister) who led lower-ranking officers, like Dalavay (commander), Vassal (guard of the palace), Rayasam (secretary/ accountant), Adaippam (personal attendant), and Kariya-karta (executive agents).

• Kingdom was divided into Rajyas or Mandalam (provinces), which were further subdivided into Nadu (district), Sthala (sub-district), and Grama (village).

o Rajyas or provinces were governed by a governor called Pradhani.

• Smaller administrative divisions like Nadu, Sima, Sthala, Kampana, etc. with the village as its smallest unit.

➢ Nayaka System (Vijayanagar Empire)

• "Nayak" denotes military chiefs in Telugu and Kannada regions.

• Revenue assigned to Nayaks for military service was present in the Kakatiya kingdom in the 13th century, which was similar to the Iqta system practiced by the Delhi sultanate. Nayaks paid a portion of revenue to the king during the Mahanavami festival.

➤ Amar-Nayak System (Vijayanagar Empire)

• It was a major political innovation of the Vijayanagara Empire.

• The Amara-nayakas were military commanders who were given territories to govern by the Raya.

• They collected taxes and other dues from peasants, craftspersons, and traders in the area. They retained part of the revenue for personal use and for maintaining a stipulated contingent of horses and elephants, providing the kings with an effective fighting force.

• Some of the revenue was used for the maintenance of temples and irrigation works.

➤ Social System (Vijayanagar Empire)

• Foreign visitors noted the opulent lifestyles of rulers, officials, and elites in cities like Vijayanagar and Bijapur, contrasting with widespread poverty and the presence of slavery. There was a widening gap between the ruling class and the ruled.

• According to Portuguese writer Nuniz, the women in the Vijayanagara Empire were experts in Wrestling, Astrology, Accounting, and Soothsaying.

➤ Economy

The tax rate varied according to the type of crops, soil, method of irrigation, etc. In addition to the land taxes, there were various other taxes, such as property tax, taxes on the sale of produce, profession taxes, military contribution (in times of distress), tax on marriage, etc.

○ These non-agrarian groups were generally called the Pattadaior (workshop people) and Kasayavargam (the group that pays taxes in cash).

○ Local communities of merchants known as Kudirai Chettis (horse merchants) also participated in these exchanges.

○ The chief gold coin of the Vijayanagar Empire was the Varaha. The Perta was half a Varaha. Fanam was one-tenth a Perta.

➤ Art and Architecture

• **Abdur Razzaq** mentioned <u>**seven lines of forts**</u> in **Hampi**, which encircled not only the city but also its agricultural hinterland and forests.

• It had its own distinct features which is called the Provida style (having a large number of pillars)

• Elaborate arrangements had been made to store rainwater: **Kamalapuram tank, Hiriya canal** (water sourced from Tungabhadra, apparently built by kings of the Sangama dynasty). The city had an elaborate canal system drawing water from the Tungabhadra.

• **Vijayanagar City** was divided into the **Sacred Centre** and the **Royal Centre.**

Mahanavami Dibba:

o Positioned atop the city's highest point, with indications of supporting a wooden structure.

o The structure likely featured rituals linked to Mahanavami, a significant day in the ten-day Hindu autumn festival (known as Dussehra in North India).

o Described as the house of victory by **Domingo Paes.**

Hazara Rama temple: Scenes from the Ramayana are sculpted on the inner walls of the shrine.

Gopurams and mandapas: Raya Gopurams or royal gateways often dwarfed the towers on the central shrines. **Kalyan Mandapas**, used for divine weddings, was a notable feature of temple construction during this period.

Virupaksha temple (Shiva Temple): Virupaksha was the guardian deity of the kingdom.

Vitthala temple (Vishnu Temple): It has several halls and a unique shrine designed as a chariot. A characteristic feature of the temple complex is the chariot street that extends from the temple gopuram in a straight line. It was also famous for Musical pillars.

3.5: Bahmani Kingdom

In **1345, Zafar Khan** declared independence <u>from the Sultanate</u> and took the title Bahaman Shah, inaugurating the Bahmani dynasty.

➤ Bahman Shah (1347–1358 AD)

• In 1345, **Bahman Shah** (also known as **Zafar Khan** and **Hasan Gangu**) declared independence at **Devagiri** and later shifted his capital to <u>Gulbarga</u> (northern Karnataka).

• He faced challenges from rulers in **Warangal, Orissa(Jajnagar)**, and **Vijayanagar**. After successful campaigns, he styled himself as the Second Alexander on coins.

• Administratively, he adopted the Delhi Sultanate's structure, dividing his realm into four regions (Gulbarga, Daulatabad, Bidar, and Berar) termed 'Tarafs'.

➤ Mohammed I (1358–1375 AD)

• Attacked **Warangal in 1363**; captured the fortress of **Golkonda** and the **Turquoise Throne**, which subsequently served as the Bahmani kings' royal seat.

• Further, he took measures for the suppression of highway robbery and built two mosques at Gulbarga.

The **Sultanate gradually broke up into four** independent kingdoms:

DYNASTY	CITY	FOUNDER
Adil Shahi	Bijapur	Yusuf Adil Shahi
Qutb Shahi	Golconda	Quli Qutub Shahi
Nizam Shahi	Ahmednagar	Malik Ahmed
Sharqi Shahi	Jaunpur	Malik Sarwar

➤ Ibrahim Adil Shah-II (1580-1627 AD)

He was the king of Bijapur. He was a good administrator, artist, Poet, and patron of arts. He also authored the book 'Kitab-i-Nauras' in Dakhani. He was given the title 'Jagadguru' by his Muslim subject because of his belief in secularism.

Mohammed I appointed a council of eight ministers of state:

Vakil-us-saltana: Lieutenant and immediate subordinate of the sovereign.

Waziri-kull: Supervised the work of all other ministers.

Amir-i-jumla: Minister of Finance

Wasir-i-ashraf: Minister of foreign affairs and Master of ceremonies.

Nazir: Assistant minister for finance

Peshwa: Associated with the lieutenant of the kingdom.

Kotwal: Chief of police and city magistrate in the capital.

Sadr-i-jahan: Chief justice and Minister of religious affairs and endowments.

Gol Gumbaz

Gol Gumbaz is the tomb of king Mohammed Adil Shah, Adil Shahi Dynasty. Construction of the tomb, located in Bijapur, Karnataka, India, was started in 1626 and was completed in 1656. The name is based on "Gol Gumbadh" derived from "Gola Gummata" meaning "circular dome".

Information →

Location **Karnataka, India**	Construction **1626**
Height **51 m**	Complete **1656**
Architects **Yaqut of Dabul**	Architectural Style **Mughal**

- **Gol Gumbad** which is said to be the largest dome in the world is situated in Bijapur district of Karnataka. It is the mausoleum of Muhammad Adil Shah (1626–1656).

- **Golkonda Fort**

o Constructed as a **mud fort by Raja Krishna Dev** of the <u>Kakatiya dynasty</u>. During 1495–1496, the fort was handed over to Sultan Kali Kutub Khan as a Jagir (land grant).

o **Qutub Shahi dynasty** took over and made Golkonda its capital.

o By the 17th century, Golkonda was famous for the 'Kohinoor' diamond.

o The Fateh Darwaza (or Victory Gate) is the entrance to the fort.

3.6: Bhakti & Sufi Movement

Bhakti tradition has been classified into **two main** categories:

• **Saguna Bhakti (with form or attributes):** The emphasis is on worshipping human-like figures of deities and their avatars. E.g.: Worship of lord Krishna by Chaitanya Mahaprabhu.

• **Nirguna Bhakti (without form or attributes):** Worship of an abstract form (nirankar) of God. Eg: God in Sikhism is formless.

Early bhakti movements around the sixth century were led by **two groups:**

○ Alvars (devotees of Vishnu): Nammalwar, Tirumangai Alwar, Andal, and Perialwar were famous Alvar saints.

○ Nayanars (devotees of Shiva): Appar, Sundarar, Thirugnana Sambandar, and Manickavachakar were famous Nayanar saints.

Key Proponents of Bhakti Movement

➤ Adi Shankaracharya (788-820 AD)

• He was born in Kaladi, Kerala. His arrival marked the beginning of philosophical Bhakti discourse in Sanskrit.

• He propounded the theory of **Advaita Vedanta (Non-Dualism)**. Sankara's Advaita, or non-dualism, had its roots in Vedanta or Upanishadic philosophy.

• His attempts to root out Buddhism and to establish smarta (traditionalist) mathas resulted in the establishment of monasteries in different places viz., Sringeri, Dvaraka, Badrinath, and Puri, which were headed by Brahmin pontiffs.

➤ Ramanuja (1017-1137 AD)

• He **challenged the monist ideology of Adi Sankara** and propounded **Vishistadvaita (Qualified Monoism).**

• Ramanuja took an interest in propagating the doctrine of Bhakti to social groups outside the varnashrama system. He influenced temple authorities to permit them to enter the temple at least once a year.

• He firmly believed that intense **devotion to Vishnu** was the best means to attain salvation. His teachings were based on the Upanishads and Bhagwad Gita and taught in a common language. He was influenced by the teachings of the Srirangam school of thought. Ramanujar joined it and was later declared the head of a monastery in Srirangam.

➤ Namdeva (1270-1350 AD)

- He came from a family of tailors. He popularised the Bhakti Movement in **Maharashtra** and was closely associated with the **Varkari Sect.**
- He was converted to the path of bhakti under the influence of Saint Janadeva.
- He wrote many **abhangs** (songs composed and sung in the glory of God) in Marathi and Hindi, and later, some of his verses were added to Guru Granth Sahib.

➤ Jnaneshwar (1275-1296 AD)

Saint of Maharashtra, revered Vishnu as Vithoba or Krishna.

- He is considered one of the most influential figures in the Varkari religious tradition.
- His poetic work on Shiva named the Ashtadasha Shiva Hikari is a poetic compilation of 18,000 verses.
- He translated the Bhagavad Gita from Sanskrit to Marathi, called Jnaneshwari.

➤ Ramananda (1400-1470 AD)

- He was a follower of Ramanuja and preached Vaishnavism in Hindi.
- He was the first to preach his doctrine of devotion in Hindi, the vernacular language.
- By establishing his own sect based on the philosophy of love and devotion to Rama and Sita, Ramananda introduced radical changes in Vaishnavism. He substituted the worship of Rama in place of Vishnu.
- He advocated equality before God and rejected the caste system, particularly the supremacy of Brahmins.
- He welcomed followers from all castes and backgrounds and had twelve chief disciples, which included Saint Kabir, Ravidas and a woman named Padmavathi.
- He famously used to say "Let no man ask a man's sect or caste".

➤ Kabir (1398-1448 AD)

- He was probably **a weaver**, born in **Varanasi**.
- Learned **Vedanta philosophy** from Swami Ramananda.
- According to Tazkirah-i-Auliya-i-Hind (Lives of Muslim Saints), he was a disciple of the Muslim Sufi, Shaikh Taqi.

• His poems express a wide range of ideas, blending Sufi and Hindu ideas like 'zikr' and 'Namsimaran' and taught that Allah and Eswar, Ram, and Rahim are one and the same.

• He had no faith in idol worship polytheism and denounced the caste system.

• He equally condemned Muslim formalism.

• Kabir's verses exist in three distinct traditions:

○ Kabir's Bijak is preserved by the Kabirpanth (the path or sect of Kabir).

○ Kabir Granthavali by Dadupanth in Rajasthan.

○ Adi Granth Sahib.

➤ Baba Guru Nanak (1469-1538 AD)

• Born in 1469, Nankana Sahib (near the Ravi river).

• Advocated **Nirguna bhakti**, believing in a formless, genderless Absolute called "rab."

• He established a community of followers and set guidelines for collective worship, or "sangat," centred on collective recitation. He founded the Sikh religion during the period of Sikander Lodi (1489-1517) and when Babur was strengthening the Mughal dynasty. [UPSC 2013]

• He dismissed rituals, sacrifices, and the scriptures of both Hindus and Muslims and emphasised connecting to the Divine by repeating the Divine Name through "shabad" hymns.

➤ Vallabhacharya (1479-1531 AD)

• Vallabhacharya, the founder of Pushtimarg (the path of grace), emphasised devotion to the child Krishna through Vatsalya Bhakti.

• He travelled across India, establishing eighty-four Pushtimarg seats during his pilgrimages.

• He propounded the theory of Shuddadvaita (pure non-dualism).

• Advocated householdership for Vaishnava devotees.

➤ Chaitanya (1485-1533 AD)

• Fondly called 'Mahaprabhu,' his songs remain popular in Bengal. He was devoted to Krishna. He started a **revivalist movement** as he wanted to exalt the superiority of Krishna over all other deities.

• His movement became popular in Bengal and Orissa.

- Considered an incarnation of Vishnu by his followers. He championed love and tolerance and opposed caste inequalities.
- He popularised 'Sankirtan' (public God-praising songs) in Bengal.

➤ Shankaradeva (1499-1569 AD)

He championed **Vaishnavism in Assam** (Especially in the Kamarupa region) through his Bhagavati dharma teachings, drawing from the Bhagavad Gita and Bhagavata Purana.

He emphasised surrendering to Vishnu and endorsed 'naam kirtan' - reciting the lord's names in devout congregations (sat sanga).

He advocated for **'satra' (monasteries) and 'naam ghar' (prayer halls)** for spiritual growth.

"Kirtana-ghosha"(written in Brajavali language) is a notable poetical composition.

He is credited for devising new forms of music i.e, Borgeet, theatrical performances like Ankia Naat and Bhaona and Sattriya dance.

➤ Tulsi Das (1532-1623 AD)

- He popularised the **Rama cult** through his Hindi rendition of Rama's story. His **notable works** include Janaki Mangal, Parvathi Mangal, Ramcharitmanas, Vinay Patrika, Dohavali, Gitavali, among others.
- He was a contemporary of Akbar and Jahangir.

➤ Tukaram (1608-1649 AD)

He was a **contemporary of Chhatrapati Shivaji, Jahangir**, Shahjahan and saints like Eknatha and Ramdas. Believed in a formless god and rejected Vedic sacrifices, pilgrimages, and idol worship.

He promoted equality and brotherhood and tried to foster Hindu-Muslim Unity. This theme is covered in a few of his verses.

He penned Abhangas in Marathi, devotional songs praising Lord Vithoba of Pandarpur.

➤ Mirabai (1498-1546 AD)

Born in Merta (Rajasthan), great-granddaughter of Rana Jodhaji, she was married to Bhoj Raj, son of Rana Sanga of Mewar. A prominent female poet in the bhakti tradition, advocating the form of Saguna bhakti. She wrote Rag-Govind.

Mirabai's guru, Raidas, was a leather worker, highlighting her rejection of caste norms.

Sufi Movement

Sufism, known as **"tasawwuf"** in Islamic texts, is the mystical dimension of Islam.

<u>Main Principles of Sufism:</u>

○ Direct communion with divine **reality (Haqiqat)** can be established by traversing the **Sufi path (tariqa)** only under the strict supervision of a shaikh, pir, or murshid.

○ Disciple (murid) progressed through the 'stages' by practising spiritual exercises such as selfmortification, recollection of God's name to attain concentration (Zikr), and contemplation.

○ The Sufis organised an impassioned musical recital (sama).

• There are many major and minor orders. Some of them were founded in India itself. The **<u>major orders</u>** are as follows.

(1) Chishtiya order   (2) Qadriya order

(3) Suharwardiya order   (4) Naqsh bandiya order

Major Teachers of the Chishti Silsila

SUFI SAINTS	Imp. Points	Location of Dargah	Time
Shaikh Muinuddin Sijzi/ Moinuddin Chishti	Came to India at the time of the Ghori conquest.	Ajmer (Rajasthan)	1143-1235
Khwaja Qutbuddin Bakhtiyar Kaki	Qutb Minar is dedicated to him.	Delhi	1173-1235
Shaikh Fariduddin Ganj-i Shakar/	Guru Granth Sahib includes hymns	Ajodhan (Pakistan)	1178–1271

Baba Farid	written by him.		
Shaikh Nizam uddin Auliya	Witnessed the reign of seven successive Sultans of Delhi.	Delhi	1238-1325
Shaikh Nasiruddin Chiragh-i Dehlavi	Also known as Roshan Chirag-e-Delhi or 'illuminated lamp of Delhi'	Delhi	1274–1337

Other Orders

➤ **Qadriya Order**

Founder: Abdul Qadir Jilani (migrated into India from the Persio-Arab land); Shah Namatullah was another saint associated with it.

Most of its followers, therefore, were staunch supporters of the very controversial theory of the unity of existence, Wahdat-ul Wujood.

Urdu poets Hasrat Mohani and Muhammad Iqbal were associated with this order.

➤ **Suharwardi Order**

Founder: Sheikh Shahabuddin Suharwardi Maqtul. He introduced the doctrine of light (Nur) into Sufism

o Bahauddin Zakarya, a contemporary of Shaikh Nizamuddin Auliya, was the most important Sufi of the Suharwardi order in India.

Unlike the Chishti saints, the Suharwardis considered the accumulation of wealth indispensable to offer better services to humanity.

➤ **Naqshbandi Order**

• Khwaja Baha-ul-din Naqsh band was the founder. Popularised by Khawja Naseer-ul-din Ubaidullah Ahrar.

• The Naqsh Bandya order was introduced in India with the invasion of Babar.

• Naqsh bandya order was less tolerant as compared to the Chishties, Qadries, and Suhawardies.

• The early Nakshbandies were inclined towards Wahadata-ul-Wadjood, the unity of existence, and the theory of Ibnul-Arabi.

• Later on, Shaikh Ahmad Sir Hindi propounded another theory known as the unity of appearance, Wahadul-ul-Shahood.

3.7: Mughal Empire & Sur Dynasty

➤ Babur (1526-1530 AD)

Babur's distinguished ancestry traces its roots to **Turko-Mongol conquerors:** <u>Timur</u> through his paternal lineage, and Mongol ruler Chengiz Khan through his maternal lineage.

<u>First Battle of Panipat (1526)</u> was fought between Babur and Ibrahim Lodi.

<u>Battle of Khanwa (1527):</u> Fought between forces of Babur on one side and Rana Sanga along with Mahmud Lodi (brother of Ibrahim Lodi) and Hasan Khan Mewati (ruler of Mewat) on the other. He later took the title of Ghazi after this war.

<u>Battle of Chanderi (1528):</u> Led to Babur's victory over Medini Rai of Chanderi in Malwa.

<u>Battle of Ghagra (1529):</u> He fought against the combined forces of Mahmud Lodi and Nusrat Shah (Bengal) along the banks of the Ghagra.

• Although gunpowder was known in India earlier, Babur exemplified its skilled use with artillery and cavalry.

• Babur introduced a **new warfare method** known as the <u>Tulguma system</u> in the first battle of Panipat. Tulughma meant dividing the whole army into various units.

• Introduced **Char Bagh** (Persian-style garden layout); Constructed mosques in Panipat and Sambhal.

• His autobiography, **Tuzuk-i-Baburi** (written in Turkish) provides an insight into his military strategies.

➤ Humayun (1530-1540 AD & 1555-1556 AD)

<u>Siege of Chunar [Mirzapur](1532):</u> He defeated the Afghans at Dardah and after that besieged Chunar fort (also known as the gateway of eastern India).

<u>Battle of Chausa[Buxar](1539):</u> Suffered defeat at the hands of Sher Shah Suri, narrowly escapingmthe battlefield.

<u>Battle of Kannauj(1540):</u> Sher Shah Suri achieved complete victory over Humayun and established an independent rule.

Humayun left India, and during his stay in <u>Amarkot</u> (Sindh, Pakistan), **Akbar was born in 1542.** Humayun then travelled to Iran, seeking assistance from its ruler, Safavid Shah.

In **1555**, Humayun won over the Afghans and reclaimed Delhi with support from Bairam Khan. In **1556**, he died due to a **fall from the staircase of his library.**

Art and Architecture

Built a **new city** in Delhi named **Dinapanah**. Constructed the **Jamali mosque** and **mosque of Isa Khan** in Delhi. His wife, **Hamida Benu Begum,** started the construction of Humayun's Tomb.

While in **Persia, Humayun** laid the foundation of **Mughal painting**, and brought notable painters Mir Sayyid Ali and Abdal Samad to India. He founded the **Nigaar Khana** (painting workshop)

He started the project of illustrating **Hamza Nama**, which was continued by Akbar.

Sher Shah Suri (Sur Empire) (1540-1555 AD)

He received the title of **Sher Khan** after **killing a tiger.**

• In **1540**, he **defeated Humayun**, marking the establishment of the second Afghan Empire in India.

• The **Conquest of Sher Shah** includes **Malwa and Ranthambore in 1542, Raisen (near Bhopal) in 1543**, Chittor in 1544, and **Kalinjar(Banda dist., UP) in 1545.**

• While besieging the Kalinjar fort in Bundelkhand in 1545, **Sher Shah died in an accidental gunpowder blast.**

Administration

• Key ministers included:

o **Diwan-i-Wizarat (Wazir)** in charge of **Revenue and Finance,**

o **Diwan-i-Ariz** overseeing the **Army,**

o **Diwan-i-Risalat** as the **Foreign Minister**, and

o **Diwan-i-Insha** handled **communications.**

• Sher Shah divided his empire into **Sarkars.** Each governed by a **Chief Shiqdar** (law and order) and a **Chief Munsif** (judge).

• **Each sarkar** was further subdivided into **several Parganas.** Each administered by a **Shiqdar** (military officer), **Amin** (land revenue officer), **Fotedar** (treasurer), and **Karkuns** (accountants).

• The **village (Mauza)** was the basic revenue unit, with hereditary chiefs collecting taxes and serving as intermediaries between the state and peasants.

- **Amin** was responsible for the construction and repair of embankments and protecting cultivable land.
- Streamlined trade imposts and collected taxes only at points of entry and sale; Standardised the metal content in gold, silver, and copper coins; Created a system of uniform weights & measures to facilitate trade; Issued a silver coin, which was termed Rupiya weighing 178 grains.
- Personal force, known as **Royal Khalsa Khail**
- **Restored Grand Trunk Road** - (Uttarapatha of ancient times): Tamralipti in Bengal to Purushpur in Peshawar and Built Sarais (rest houses) on the trade routes.
- Construction of a **new walled city in Delhi**, known as **Purana Qila (Old Fort)**, and Built his **own mausoleum** in **Sasaram.**
- Imposed Jaziya on the Hindus.

Akbar (1556-1605 AD)

Bairam Khan was Akbar's tutor and his most trusted ally. He served as a regent from 1556-60 AD.

Second Battle of Panipat (1556): Hemu and the Afghan forces were defeated by the Mughal forces under Akbar.

Gujarat (1573): From Muzaffar Shah, later Gujarat became a launch pad for the annexation of Deccan.

Battle of Haldighati (1576): Akbar secured a decisive win in the Battle of Haldighati where Maharana Pratap suffered severe defeat at the hands of the Mughal army under Man Singh.

Administration of Akbar

Divided empire into 12 provinces (suba), endowing each with a Diwan, Bakshi, Sadr, and Qazi who replicated the functions of their central counterparts. Provinces were further subdivided into sarkars and Parganas.

Suba (Province):

○ Headed by a Subedar responsible for law and order.
○ Diwan managed revenue, supervised collections, and increased cultivation.
○ Taccavi (loans) to peasants were facilitated through revenue department.
○ Bakshi oversaw horses and soldiers.

○ Sadar represented central authority, overseeing religious and judicial matters.

Sarkar (District):

○ Headed by Faujdar who took care of rebellions and law and order problems, protecting residents and assisting in revenue collection.

○ Amalguzar/Amil was the most important revenue collector. A good amil was supposed to increase the land under cultivation and induce the peasants to pay revenue willingly without coercion.

Pargana:

○ Headed by Shiqdar (executive officer) who assisted Amalguzar in revenue collection.

○ Quanungo maintained land records.

○ Kotwals, appointed in towns, maintained law and order.

Village:

○ Headed by Muqaddam (village headman).

○ Patwari managed village revenue records

○ Zamindars assisted in law and order and revenue collection.

○ Forts were administered by a Qiladar.

Land Revenue System

• Land Revenue Arrangements include **two stages** of revenue collection:

○ Assessment (Jama) and Actual collection (Hasil).

○ **Zabt/Zabti** System (enforced by Sher Shah and adopted by Akbar), associated with **Raja Todar Mal**, also called Todar Mal's Bandobast.

• The **Dahsala System**, introduced in **1580 AD**, calculated revenue based on the average yield of the past ten years, factoring in local prices. **Parganas** with similar productivity were organised into distinct assessment circles.

• Land was categorised into the following with their respective assessment rates: **Polaj** (under cultivation almost every year); **Parati** (uncultivated land); **Chachar** (fallow for two to three years), **Banjar** (fallow more than five years) and **Karoris** were appointed for collection and audit of revenue.

• **Amils** (revenue collectors) were encouraged **to support peasants** by providing **Taccavi loans** for diverse needs and enabling repayment in manageable instalments.

Architecture

Agra Fort was constructed using red sandstone. Inside Agra Fort, Akbar built the **Jahangiri Mahal**, incorporating Hindu design principles inspired by the Man Mandir.

Fatehpur Sikri (The City of Victory): It is a **UNESCO** World Heritage Site. It includes:

○ **Buland Darwaza** (built after the victory over Gujarat in 1572), **Jama Masjid, Jodha Bai's palace**, the **Panch Mahal** designed akin to a Buddhist Vihara, the **Diwan-i-Khas**, the **Diwan-i-Aam**, and **Sheikh Salim Chisti's tomb.**

Religion

• Akbar married **Harkha Bai** (daughter of Raja Bhar Mal of Amber) and princesses from Bikaner and Jaisalmer.

• Construction of **Ibadat Khana** (Hall of Prayers) at Fatehpur Sikri

• Akbar introduced a new religion called **Din-i-Ilahi or Tauhind-i-Ilahi (Divine Monotheism) in 1582.** It emphasised belief in one God and "Sulh-i-Kul" incorporating positive aspects from various religions with a rational foundation as documented by Badayuni. Despite efforts, Din-i-Ilahi did not gain widespread acceptance and gradually faded after Akbar's demise.

Art & Literature

• **Akbar Nama** was compiled by **Abul Fazl**. It contained three volumes of the history of Akbar's reign. **Ain-i-Akbari** deals with Akbar's administration, army, revenues, and geography of his empire.

• Mahabharata, renamed **'Razmnama' (Book of Wars)** was translated into Persian. It was completed in 1589 under the supervision of master artist Daswant.

• Prominent painters: **Daswant and Basawan.**

• **Madonna and Child (1580)** by Baswan is an important work of the Mughal School of Painting. Akbar Hamzanama (best known for the enormous illustrated manuscript).

➢ **Jahangir (1605-1627 AD)**

Nur-ud-din Jahangir, known as 'Salim' after Sufi saint Sheikh Salim Chishti. He was born to the Rajput princess Mariam-uz-Zamani (also known by the name Jodha Bai).

His Persian wife Mehrunnisa, renamed Nur-Jahan by Jahangir, became the real power behind the throne. Coins were issued in her name, and she was given the title of Badshah Begum.

Administration

He added the "duh-aspah-sih-aspah" system, a modification of the Mansabdari system, where a Mansabdar could maintain a larger cavalry without raising his zat rank.

○ Duh-aspah - a trooper with two horses.

○ Sih-aspah - a trooper with three horses.

He introduced 'Zanjeer-E-Adal' (chain of justice).

Art & Literature

• **Moti Masjid** was built by Jahangir in Lahore.

• **Shalimar Garden** was constructed in Kashmir.

• Under Jahangir, the Mughal paintings achieved naturalism and scientific accuracy of the highest degree.

○ He was particularly interested in the portrait style. He introduced the **use of halos** (circular divine light behind the head) in portraits during his reign.

○ The **Muraqqas** (individual paintings to be mounted in albums) became popular.

• Jahangir wrote his auto-biography **Tuzuk-i-Jahangiri** in **Persian.**

➤ Shah Jahan (1628-1658 AD)

Under his emperorship, the Mughals reached the peak of their architectural achievements and cultural glory.

Deccan: Launched campaign against Ahmadnagar, Bijapur, and Golconda.

North-west: the campaign to seize Balkh from the **Uzbegs** was unsuccessful and **Qandahar** was lost to the Safavids. Afghan noble Khan Jahan Lodi rebelled and was defeated.

Bundelas were defeated and Orchha seized.

Administration

There was an exceptional increase in the number of mansabdars, consuming more than threefourths of the revenues of the state. The highest form of submission Sijda (complete prostration) was replaced with Chahar Taslim (mode of salutation done four times) and Zaminbos (kissing the ground).

Architecture & Literature

• The Mughal Empire reached its **architectural zenith** under **Shah Jahan. In 1631, Shah Jahan started** the construction of the <u>Taj Mahal</u> in memory of his wife, **Mumtaz Mahal (Arjumand Bano Begum)**. It was **completed in 1648.**

• During Shah Jahan's reign mosque-building flourished, with notable constructions including: **Moti Masjid in Agra** (crafted entirely in white marble); **Sheesh Mahal and Mussaman Burj in Agra**; and Jama **Masjid in Delhi** was built using red stone.

• Shah Jahan's reign saw the pinnacle of fort-building, which included the <u>Red Fort in Delhi</u> with the Rang Mahal, Diwan-i-Aam, and Diwan-i-Khas.

• **Shah Jahan is also credited** with the construction of <u>Shalimar Bagh</u> in **Lahore** and the establishment of the **city of Shahjahanabad.**

• The famous **Peacock Throne** in the **Diwan-i-Khas** (Hall of Private Audiences, or Ministers' Room) in the Red Fort of Delhi was built for Shah Jahan.

• Inayat Khan authored 'Shah Jahan Nama.' (an unillustrated chronicle of the reign of Shah Jahan)

• His court historian **Abdul Hameed Lahori** authored **'Badshah Nama.'** (an illustrated group of works written as the official history of the reign of Shah Jahan)

➤ **Aurangzeb (1658-1707 AD)**

Aurangzeb (Alamgir, "World Conqueror") rose to power in 1658. His reign of fifty years falls into two equal parts:

o **First twenty-five years:** He resided in the north, chiefly at Delhi, and personally occupied himself with the affairs of northern India, leaving the Deccan in the hands of his Viceroys.

o **Around 1681:** He was prompted by the rebellion of one of his sons, Prince Akbar, to go to the Deccan. He never returned to Delhi, died at Ahmad Nagar in 1707.

Religious Views

• Strict religious policy marginalising non-Muslims led to various uprisings: **Jat rebellion** in 1669 and 1685; **Satnami rebellion** in 1672; **Execution of the ninth Sikh Guru Tegh Bahadur**, which led to the Sikh rebellion in 1675.

• Prohibited court music, drinking of wine, and use of opium.

• **Reinstated Jizya** and **pilgrimage tax** on Hindus

• He dismissed court musicians and royal painters and discontinued the practice of Jharokha darshan.

• He replaced the **Solar calendar** with the **Hijra calendar** under the Influence of Nakshabandi Sufi order.

• Muhtasibs were appointed to uphold **moral codes and sharia.**

• **Discontinued "abwab,"** a tax levied on the lands over and above the original rent.

• For rigorous adherence to **Islamic principles**, he was often referred to as **Zinda Pir** (living saint).

Mughal Administration

Khalisa	land owned by the emperor directly
Jagir	Given to Mansabdrs as salary.
Inam	Assigned to learned and religious men.
Wazir or Diwani-ala	Headed the revenue department but did not hold a high mansab.
Mir Saman	In charge of the imperial household, managing supplies and provisions.
Sadr-us-Sudur	He was the head of the ecclesiastical department.
Mir Bakshi	Head of military administration, overseeing armed contingents and war equipment. He personally supervised the branding of the horses (Dagh) and checked the muster-roll (Chehra) of the soldiers.

Mansabdari System

The term **"mansabdar"** referred to an individual who held mansab, meaning a position or rank. It was a grading system used by the Mughals to fix (1) rank, (2) salary, and (3) military responsibilities.

• Rank and salary were determined by a numerical value called zat.

• The mansabdar's military responsibilities required him to maintain a specified number of sawar or cavalrymen.

○ Mansabdars received their salaries as revenue assignments called jagirs.

○ Jagirs were subject to regular transfers and were not hereditary. Further, these were reverted to the state upon Mansabdar's death.

Akbar's Navratanas: Akbar's court was said to have a group of intellectuals known as the Navaratnas.

Abul Fazl	Royal court historian who wrote Akbar Nama.
Faizi(RajKavi)	Persian poet and elder brother of Abul Fazl.
FakirAziaoDin	A Sufi mystic and a key advisor to Akbar.
Tansen (Ramatanu Pandey)	Renowned musician, a court musician to King Ramachandra, who accepted Islam under Sufi mystic Muhammad Ghaus of Gwalior. Tansen was the title given to him by Raja Vikramjit of Gwalior. Akbar bestowed upon him the name "Mian".
Birbal (Kavi Priya)	A courtier, bestowed with the titles Raja and Birbal by Akbar. Died fighting Yusuf Shahis on the Northwest frontiers.
Raja Todar Mal (Diwan-i-Ashraf)	Finance minister overseeing the revenue system. Introduced standard weights, measurements, and revenue districts.
Raja Man Singh	A Mansabdar, the grandson of Akbar's father-in-law.
Abdul Rahim Khan-iKhanan	A great poet; translated Babarnama into Turki, Son of Bairam Khan.
Mulla Do-Piyaza	Advisor and Wazir of the Mughal emperor Akbar.

The Later Mughals

➤ **Bahadur Shah I (1707-1712 AD)**

Mughal historians have entitled him **"Shah-i-Bekhabar,"** due to his administrative inefficiency. Demonstrated **tolerance towards Hindus**, although he **didn't abolish the jizya tax.**

Initiated peace with Guru Gobind Singh, but subsequent Sikh rebellions post the Guru's death saw him leading campaigns against the Sikhs.

➤ Jahandar Shah (1712-1713 AD)

• After Bahadur Shah's death, Mughal politics changed, with **nobles becoming the king-makers** and the emperors becoming their puppets. Jahandar Shah emerged as the first puppet ruler, with **Zulfiqar Khan(Wazir)** holding real power.

• He ordered the **abolition of the Jizya** tax.

➤ Farruk Siyar (1713-1719 AD)

He came to power with the help of the **Sayyid brothers**, Abdullah Khan (Wazir) and Husain Ali Khan Baraha (Mir Bakshi).

In **1717 AD, Farrukh Siyar** granted significant **trading privileges** to the East India Company and exempted customs duties for their trade through Bengal.

➤ Muhammad Shah (Rangeela) (1719-1748 AD)

• He ousted the **Sayyid brothers** around **1720.**

Under his reign, several states declared independence: **Nizam-ul-Mulk** ruling the Deccan; Saadat Khan leading Awadh; and Murshid Quli Khan governing Bihar, Bengal, and Orissa.

• The fragility of the <u>Mughal Empire</u> was exposed when **Nadir Shah invaded India** around 1739 AD.

➤ Alamgir II (1754-1759 AD)

The famous **Battle of Plassey,** 1757 AD, took place during his reign.

This battle facilitated the British East India Company's takeover of Bengal.

➤ Shah Alam II (1759-1806 AD)

• In 1764, he, alongside Mir Qasim and Shuja-ud-Daula, waged war against the English East India Company but faced defeat at the **Battle of Buxar.**

• Subsequently, he resided in **Allahabad as a British pensioner (first one) until 1772**, when he returned to Delhi under Maratha protection.

➤ Akbar II (1806-1837 AD)

He reigned under British protection post-1803 AD capture of Delhi by the British, noted for bestowing the title of **"Raja"** upon Ram Mohan Roy.

Acknowledged as a distinguished poet, initiated the **Phool Walon Ki Sair**, promoting Hindu-Muslim unity.

➢ Bahadur Shah II (1837-1857 AD)

• Last Mughal Emperor and celebrated Urdu poet under the pen name "Zafar."

• Played a pivotal role in the **1857 Revolt** and was proclaimed the Emperor of India by the rebels.

• Post-revolt, he faced **exile in Rangoon** (modern-day Myanmar) and **died there in 1862**.

3.8: Marathas & Maratha Confederacy

They were a mix of various agrarian castes who distinguished themselves by their military service traditions, earning land grants in return.

They **served in the armies** of the **Bahamani kingdom** and successor states. Bijapur rulers like Ibrahim Adil Shah used them as a counterbalance to their Deccani and Afaqi units.

➢ Chatrapati Shivaji (1627–1680 AD)

• At a young age, he acquired the Torna fort from Bijapur Sultan in 1646. Further, he captured and rebuilt the Raigad Fort. He took control of the forts of Baramati, Indapura, Purandhar, and Kondana.

• In **1656**, he became popular as he **wrested Javali (Satara district)** from its **Maratha chief**, took control of the highlands (Maval region) and constructed the **Pratapgarh fort.**

• Recognising naval significance, he built a naval fleet to confront the Sidis of Janjira, who managed several ports and had a large navy; he couldn't overpower them due to ineffective artillery.

Key Military Conquests

Shivaji attacked the Bijapur, occupying northern Konkan. This provoked Ali Adil Shah II to send General Afzal Khan in 1659, whose forces desecrated Hindu sites, including the revered Pandharpur.

Shivaji responded by killing Afzal Khan, followed by seizing of Panhala fort and territories in southern Konkan and Kolhapur.

1664: Shivaji plundered Surat, a significant Mughal port, prompting Aurangzeb to deploy Raja Jai Singh to counter him and capture Bijapur. With a comprehensive encirclement, Shivaji was forced to negotiate, paving the way for the Treaty of Purandar in 1665.

According to the **treaty of Purandhar:**

○ Shivaji had to surrender 23 forts to the Mughals.

○ He was to serve as Mughal Mansabdar and join the Mughals against Bijapur.

○ The Mughals recognised the right of Shivaji to hold certain parts of the Bijapur kingdom.

○ As Shivaji was exempted from personal service of the Mughals, his minor son Sambhaji was granted a Mansab of 5000 zat.

1666: Jai Singh persuaded Shivaji to visit the Mughal court in Agra, where he faced disrespect and humiliation. He was put under house arrest, which he successfully escaped.

1670: Aurangzeb reclaimed a portion of Shivaji's jagir in Berar. Shivaji retaliated by withdrawing his troops from the Mughal service, reclaimed the forts surrendered in the Treaty of Purandar and raided Surat again.

By **1672, the Marathas imposed a Chauth** (one-fourth of the revenue) as an annual tribute on Surat.

Coronation

In **1674**, Shivaji was crowned at Raigarh, assuming the title of **"Chhatrapathi" (supreme king)**. The day of his consecration marked the commencement of a new era, the Rajyabhisheka saka.

He described himself as "the protector of cows and brahmins" (gobrahmance pratipalak) and "the upholder of dharma" (dharma parayena).

Maratha Administration

Shivaji had **an advisory council** called **'Ashta Pradhan Mandal'** with **eight ministers.**

Mukhya Pradhan (Peshwa)	He was the prime minister and looked after the general welfare and interests of the State and officiated for the king in his absence.
Amatya/Mazumdar	Finance minister.
Walkia-Nawis (Mantri)	Maintained the records of the king's activities and the proceedings in the court.
Summant (Dabir or foreign secretary)	Advised on war, peace, and diplomacy.
Sachiv (Shuru Nawis)	Managed correspondence with the king and checked accounts of Parganas.

Pandit Rao (Danadhyaksha)	Oversaw religion, ceremonies, and morality.
Nyayadhish	The chief justice responsible for civil and military justice.
Sari Naubat (Senapati)	The commander-in-chief.

Administration

• Shivaji controlled the influential Maratha landed families (Deshmukhs) by expanding the crown land.

• **Adnyapatra** was a royal edict on the principles of **Maratha policy** written in **Modi script** by Ramchandra Pant Amatya.

• Shivaji divided the kingdom (Swaraj) into Mauzas, Tarafs and Prants.

o **Provinces** were known as prants under subedar, karkun (or mukhya desbadhikari).

o **Tarfs** were headed by a havaldar, karkunoa paripatyagar.

o **Mauza** was the smallest unit.

• The police officer in the **rural area** was called **Faujdar** and in the **urban area** was called **Kotwal.**

Economy

The revenue system was established on **Malik Amber's Kathi system,** where the land was calculated by **Rod or Kathi.**

Shivaji's revenue system was compassionate to farmers, with lands diligently assessed and a **fixed** state demand of **initially 30%,** later **raised to 40%,** of the gross produce.

Chauth and Sardeshmukhi: Shivaji collected **Chauth** (one-fourth of the revenue of the district conquered) and **Sardeshmukhi** (an additional 10% by virtue of his position as Sardeshmukh) from adjoining territories of his empire, conquered territories, and Mughal/Bijapur lands.

Military

• The Marathas were **experts in guerrilla warfare**, along with the use of an innovative weapon, the **Bagh naka**, meaning tiger claw.

• The infantry was highly mobile and light, with **Mavli** (foot soldiers) playing an important role.

• The smallest unit, with nine soldiers, was headed by a **Naik** (corporal). Each unit with **25 horsemen** was placed under one **Havildar** (equivalent to the rank of a sergeant). **Five havildars** were placed under one Jamaladar, and ten Jamaladars under one Hazari.

• The cavalry was divided into two classes: **Bargirs** (soldiers whose horses were given by the state) and **Shiledars** (mercenary horsemen who had to find their own horses).

Marathas Under Peshwa

➤ Balaji Viswanath (1713–1720 AD)

He helped **Maratha emperor Shahu** stabilise the kingdom after the civil war; Convinced Kanhoji Angre to support Shahu against Europeans; Revived jagir grants and made Peshwa's office hereditary.

➤ Baji Rao I (1720–1740 AD)

He was the **most famous** of **all nine Peshwas** and also known as **"Thorale"**, meaning 'Elder' Baji Rao.

• He was the greatest exponent of **guerrilla tactics** after Shivaji.

• He shifted the administrative capital from **Satara to Pune** in 1728 AD.

• He **initiated** the system of **confederacy** among the Maratha chiefs.

• Popularised the idea of Hindu-padpadshahi (Hindu Empire) to secure the support of Hindu chiefs against the Mughals.

• Defeated Nizam of Hyderabad, the Rajput Governor of Malwa, and the Governor of Gujarat.

➤ Balaji Baji Rao (1740–1761 AD)

• During his reign, **Maratha king Shahu died in 1749 AD** and his nominated successor, Ramraja, was imprisoned by the Peshwa at Satara. Thus, the supreme power of the Maratha confederacy **passed into the hands of Peshwa** (by the Sangola Agreement of 1750 AD).

- He defeated the Nawab of Bengal, Alivardi Khan, and agreed with the Mughal Emperor in 1752 AD.

Administration of the Peshwas

- Peshwa was one of Shivaji's Ashta Pradhan (council of ministers). The office was initially not hereditary but gained prominence as the king's power declined.
- The centre of the Maratha administration was the Peshwa Secretariat at Poona.
- Large provinces had Sar-Subahdars as provincial governors. Divisions in the provinces were called Subahs and Pranths.
- Mamlatdar and Kamavistar were Peshwa's representatives in the districts and were responsible for every branch of district administration.
- Deshmukh and Deshpandes, who were district officers in charge of accounts observed the activities of Mamlatdars and Kamavistars. It was a system of checks and balances.
- The village was the basic unit of administration headed by Patel and was self-supportive.
- The Patel (not paid by the government and hereditary chief officer) was responsible for remitting revenue to the centre, assisted by the accountant and record-keeper, Kulkarni.
- Kotwal was the chief officer in towns and cities. He also functioned as the magistrate.

Economy

Land revenue was the primary income that transitioned from the sharing of agricultural produce (Shivaji's time) to tax farming.

Assessment of land revenue was based on the kinds of crops, facilities for irrigation, and productivity of the land.

Others

- Watchmen were employed in every village. They were usually from the Mahar caste.
- They recruited soldiers from across India, contrasting with Shivaji's local Maratha enlistment.
- They guarded Maratha ports, combated piracy, and collected customs duties. Balaji Vishwanath established naval bases at Konkan, Khanderi, and Vijayadurg.

3.9: Foreign Travellers in Medieval India

PERIOD (century)	TIMELINE	RELATED RULERS	TRAVELLERS (COUNTRY)
10th	914-928	Rashtrakuta, Gurjara-Pratihara	Al-Masudi(Iraq)
	973-1048	Mahmud of Ghazni	Al-Biruni (Uzbekistan)
	940-1019		Firdausi(Iran) - "Homer of the East"
13th	1227	Slave Dynasty (Sultanate)	Minhaj - us - Siraj (Iran)
	1292-93	Pandyas	Marco Polo (Italy)
14th	1304-77	Md. Bin Tughlaq	Ibn Battuta (Morocco)
15th	1420	Deva Raya II (Vijayanagar)	Niccolò de' Conti(Italy)
	1440s		Abdur Razzaq Samarqandi (Uzbekistan)
	1469	Bahmani	Afanasii Nikitich Nikitin (Russia)
	1518	Vijayanagar	Duarte Barbosa, d.1521 (Portugal)
16th	1520	Krishnadev Raya	Domingo Paes(Portugal)
	1536-1600	Akbar	Antonio Monserrate (Spain)
	1600-67	Shah Jahan	Peter Mundy (England)
17th	1605-89	Shah Jahan and Aurangzeb	Jean-Baptiste Tavernier (France)
	1620-88	Aurangzeb	François Bernier (France)

3.10: Books & Authors from Medieval India

BOOK	AUTHOR	DETAILS
• Prashnottara Ratnamalika • Kavirajamarga	Amoghavarsha I	Key works in Sanskrit and Kannada.
Prithviraj Raso	Chandbardai	Biography: Prithviraj Chauhan
Prithviraj Vijaya	Jayanaka	The account of Prithviraj Chauhan's reign
Tajul-Ma'asir	Hasan Nizami	It is the earliest among the historical literature produced in India
Tughlaq Nama	Amir Khusrau	It is a biography of Ghiyasuddin along with other Tughlaq rulers

Fatuhat-i-Firozshahi	Firoz Shah Tughlaq	Autobiography of Firoz Shah Tughlaq
Tarikh-i-Firozshahi Fatawa-i-Jahandari	Zia-ud-Din Barani	Exemplified the art of Persian prose writing Key accounts of Tughlaq Rule
Tabaqat-i-Nasari	Minhaj-us-Siraj	A comprehensive history of Muslim dynasties up to 1260 AD
Tutinama	Zia Nakshabi	Tales of a Parrot, a series of short stories
Gulshan-i Ibrahimi or Tarikh-i Firishta	Ferishta	It provided a traditional narrative of events and dynasties from the times of the Ghaznavid ruler Mahmud (early 11th century) until the time of Firishta's patron, the Sultan of Bijapur Ibrahim Adil Shah II.
Kitab-i-Nauras	Ibrahim Adil Shah-II	It is a collection of songs in praise of Hindu deities and Muslim saints
Tuzuk-i-Baburi (Baburanamah)	Babur	Autobiography of Babur
Humayun-Nama	Gul Badan Begum	Key account of Humayun's life and rule
Akbar Nama	Abul Fazl	It contained three volumes of the history of Akbar's reign
Tuzuk-i-Jahangiri	Jahangir	Autobiography of Jahangir
Shah Jahan Nama	Inayat Khan	An unillustrated chronicle of the reign of Shah Jahan
Badshah Nama	Abdul Hameed Lahori	An illustrated group of works written as the official history of the reign of Shah Jahan

4. Modern Indian History

4.1: The Advent of Europeans in India

➤ The Portuguese

Portuguese become the <u>**first to reach India**</u>. Prince **Henry of Portugal**, also known as the **'Navigator'** was given a bull by **Pope Nicholas V** in 1454, conferring on him the right to explore the oriental shores as far as India.

<u>**Vasco Da Gama**</u> visited India three times - 1498, 1501 and 1524.

Pedro Alvarez Cabral embarked on a voyage to trade for spices and established **a factory in Calicut** in September 1500.

In 1505, the King of Portugal appointed **Francisco De Almeida** as governor of India. He aimed to make the Portuguese the master of the Indian Ocean, implementing the **Blue Water Policy (Cartaze system).**

Alfonso de Albuquerque succeeded Almeida as Portuguese Governor in India and is considered to be the real founder of Portuguese power in the East. He introduced a **'permit system'** for other ships.

➢ Acquired <u>**Goa from Sultan of Bijapur in 1510**</u>, which became the first Indian territory under European control since Alexander the Great.

➢ Introduced new crops like Tobacco and Cashew nut, or better plantation varieties of coconut.

➢ Albuquerque abolished sati and encouraged Portuguese men to marry locals.

➤ The Dutch

Cornelis de Houtman was the first Dutchman to reach Sumatra and Bantam in 1596.

The **Dutch** founded their **first factory** in **Masulipatnam (in Andhra) in 1605.**

Important Dutch factories were in Surat (1616), Bimlipatam (1641), Karaikal (1645), Chinsura (1653), Baranagar, Kasimbazar (near Murshidabad), Balasore, Patna, Nagapatam (1658), and Cochin (1663).

The **Dutch monopolized trade in black pepper and spices**. They were also interested in silk, cotton, indigo, rice and opium.

➤ The English

• Queen **Elizabeth I** of England grants a formal charter to the London merchants trading with the East Indies.

• <u>**Captain Hawkins**</u> came to the court of **Jahangir in 1609** with the aim of establishing a factory and gaining trade concessions.

• In **1611**, the English **began trading** at <u>**Masulipatnam and established a factory there in 1616**</u>.

• <u>**Captain Thomas Best defeated the Portuguese in 1612**</u> off the coast of Surat, leading to Jahangir granting permission to the English to establish a **factory at Surat in 1613**.

• **Sir Thomas Roe** arrived in 1615 and stayed until February 1619. Though unsuccessful in concluding a commercial treaty with Jahangir, Roe secured several privileges, including the permission to set up factories at Agra, Ahmedabad, and Broach.

• In 1639, the ruler of Chandragiri (representatives of Vijayanagara Empire) gave permission to build a fortified factory at Madras, which later became Fort St. George and replaced Masulipatnam as the English headquarters in South India.

➤ The Danes (Denmark)

The Danish East India Company was established in 1616, and they founded their **first factory at Tranquebar** near Tanjore in 1620.

Serampore near Calcutta was the most important Danish settlement at the time. The Danes were more interested in missionary activities, instead of commercial or political interests.

➤ The French

• The French were the last Europeans to arrive in India with the purpose of trade.

• Compagnie des Indes Orientales (French East India Company) was established by Minister Colbert in **1664** during the reign of Louis XIV.

• The **first French Factory** in India was established by Francois Caron in <u>**Surat in 1667**</u>. Mercara, a Persian who accompanied Caron, founded another French factory in Masulipatnam in 1669 after obtaining a patent from the Sultan of Golconda.

• **Important French centre:** Mahe, Karaikal, Balasore, Chandernagore near Calcutta, Pondicherry.

The Carnatic Wars: Anglo-French Struggle for Supremacy

> ### First Carnatic War (1740-48)

It was an **extension of the Anglo-French War** in Europe caused by the Austrian War of Succession.

Ended in 1748 with the signing of the **Treaty of Aix-La Chapelle.**

> ### Second Carnatic War (1749-54)

The war was caused by the succession struggles after the death of Nizam-ul-Mulk, wherein the **French supported** the claims of **Muzaffar Jang and Chanda Sahib** in the Deccan and Carnatic, respectively, while the **English sided with Nasir Jang and Anwaruddin.**

The **Treaty of Pondicherry**, which was signed in 1754 and recognized Muhammad Ali Khan Walajah as the Nawab of the Carnatic, put an end to the Second Carnatic War.

> ### Third Carnatic War

• Started as a result of the **Seven Years' War in Europe,** which had its effects on Anglo-French rivalry in India.

• **Battle of Wandiwash (1760):** The decisive battle of the Third Carnatic War was won by the English on January 22, 1760, at Wandiwash (or Vandavasi) in Tamil Nadu.

• General Eyre Coote of the English totally routed the French army under Count Thomas Arthur de Lally.

• The **Treaty of Peace of Paris (1763)** restored the French factories, but their political influence disappeared after the war.

4.2: Expansion and Consolidation of British Power in India

The Battle of Plassey (1757): The 'Black-Hole Tragedy' increased friction between the British and Sirajud-Daulah. Robert Clive forged a secret alliance with Mir Jafar, Jagat Seth and others who were traitors to the Nawab. The English won the battle easily due to the conspiracy.

Mir Jafar became the Nawab of Bengal, and he gave the English Zamindari of the 24 parganas along with money. The English posted a resident at Nawab's court, and their sovereignty over Calcutta was recognised.

The Battle of Buxar (1764): The company misused its Dastaks (trade permits) which caused financial loss to the Nawab and thus led to tensions.

• Major Hector Munro led the English forces and gained a decisive victory over Mir Kasim and his allies.

• The **Treaty of Allahabad, 1765** was concluded by Robert Clive with the Nawab of Awadh and Shah Alam II.

• Nawab Shuja-ud-Daula agreed to surrender Allahabad and Kara to Emperor Shah Alam II.

• **Shah Alam II** agreed to reside at Allahabad, to be ceded to him by the Nawab of Awadh, under the Company's protection, and **issue a Farman granting the Diwani of Bengal, Bihar, and Orissa** to the East India Company.

Dual Government in Bengal (1765-72): Introduced by Robert Clive, wherein both the Company and the Nawab ruled. The Company had both Nizamat and Diwani rights. Warren Hastings abolished the Dual Government System.

ANGLO-MYSORE WARS

➤ **First Anglo-Mysore War (1767-69)**

Haidar Ali attacked Madras and caused the English to conclude the Treaty of Madras with favourable outcomes for Mysore.

➤ **Second Anglo-Mysore War (1780-84)**

Haidar formed an alliance with the Marathas and the Nizam against the English. He attacked the Carnatic, capturing Arcot and defeating the English army led by Colonel Baillie in 1781. The English, under **Sir Eyre Coote**, managed to detach the Marathas and the Nizam from Haidar's alliance. Haidar faced the English again and suffered a defeat at Porto Novo in November 1781.

In 1782, Haidar Ali succumbed to cancer, leading his son, Tipu Sultan, to carry on the war for another year with no decisive outcome.

The Treaty of Mangalore, signed in March 1784, facilitated the return of territories taken by each side during the hostilities.

➤ **Third Anglo-Mysore War (1792)**

A dispute between Tipu and the state of Travancore turned into a war, with the English siding with Travancore. The English attacked Seringapatam and succeeded in their attack.

The Treaty of Seringapatam (1792) resulted in territorial changes, with the English gaining control of Baramahal, Dindigul, and Malabar.

➢ Fourth Anglo-Mysore War (1799)

• Tipu declared himself Sultan once the Hindu ruler of the **Wodeyar dynasty** died and sought to avenge his humiliation by the British.

• **Lord Wellesley, the new Governor General**, was concerned about Tipu's friendship with the French and sought to punish him.

• Tipu faced defeats at the hands of English Generals Stuart and Harris. The English received support from the Marathas and the Nizam.

• A boy from the previous Hindu royal family of Mysore was appointed as the new maharaja, subjected to the subsidiary alliance system.

ANGLO-MARATHA WAR

➢ First Anglo-Maratha War (1775-82)

The Maratha succession conflict led to Sawai Madhavrao's endorsement over Raghunath Rao.

The treaty of Surat ceded Salsette and Bassein to English. Treaty violations led to war, resulting in the Treaty of Wadgaon.

Hastings disapproved the Treaty of Wadgaon, leading to the Treaty of Salbai after defeating Sindhia.

➢ Second Anglo-Maratha War (1803-05)

Maratha's disunity facilitated English intrusion. Bajirao II signed the Treaty of Bassein, ceding Surat and accepting troops. The treaty restricted European employment and subjected relations to English oversight.

Scindia and Bhonsle resisted and were defeated by the English, signing the Surji-Anjangaon and Devgaon treaties. Holkar defeat led to the Rajpurghat Treaty.

➢ Third Anglo-Maratha War (1817-19)

• Lord Hastings sought to establish British paramountcy, prompted by the termination of the East India Company's trade monopoly in China, except for tea, by the Charter Act of 1813.

• Friction arose from Pindari raids on Company territories, attributed to Maratha support.

• The Treaty of Bassein, perceived as a capitulation to British control, angered other Maratha leaders. Bajirao II led a Maratha attack on

Nagpur, but the weakened Maratha administration led to their defeat by the British.

• Subsequent treaties were signed with the defeated Maratha factions, leading to the dissolution of the Maratha confederacy in 1818.

ANGLO-SIKH WARS

❖ First Anglo-Sikh War (1845-46)

The war arose from the Sikh army crossing the River Sutlej, turmoil following Maharaja Ranjit Singh's death, English military actions in Afghanistan and annexations, and heightened English military presence near Lahore.

British manipulation led to Sikh defeats, Lahore's fall, and the Treaty of Lahore's humiliating terms.

Subsequent unrest, including the sale of Kashmir to Gulab Singh, sparked further rebellion and the signing of the Treaty of Bhairowal.

❖ Second Anglo-Sikh War (1848-49)

Sikh grievances over humiliating treaty terms, mistreatment of Rani Jindan, and Mulraj's rebellion led to the Second Anglo-Sikh War.

Lord Dalhousie seized the opportunity to annex Punjab, winning battles led by Sir Hugh Gough. The Sikh army surrendered at Rawalpindi. Dalhousie's objective was completed with Punjab's annexation and governance by a three-member board.

John Lawrence later became Punjab's first chief commissioner.

Other British Policies

The Policy of Ring Fence: Warren Hastings devised this policy with the aim to create buffer zones to defend the Company's frontiers.

The states included in the ring-fence system were guaranteed military support against outside aggression, albeit at their own cost.

Subsidiary Alliance: Lord Wellesley used the subsidiary alliance system, an extension of the Ring Fence policy, to build an empire in India between 1798-1805.

However, it was Dupleix who first used the system of Subsidiary alliance. Under the system, Indian rulers had to agree to permanent British military presence and payment, and the placement of a British resident in their courts. The Indian emperor needed Company approval for hiring Europeans and had to consult the governor general for warfare or diplomacy with other rulers. In return, the British guaranteed protection and non-interference in internal affairs.

Awadh was the first Indian state to fall victim to this protection trap.

Doctrine of Lapse: Lord Dalhousie used this policy and was able to annex multiple states.

The doctrine, to put it simply, said that the adopted son might inherit his foster father's private property but not the state.

States that were subjected to this: Satara (1848), Nagpur and Jhansi (1854), and The other small states were Baghat (Himachal Pradesh), Sambhalpur (Orissa), and Jaitpur (Bundelkhand).

4.3: People's Resistance against British before 1857

➤ Sanyasi Revolt (1763-1800) [Bihar & Bengal]

It was a revolt by the **Sannyasis and Sadhus** in Bengal. It was characterized by equal participation of Hindus and Muslims. It is also known as the **Fakir Rebellion**. They raided Company factories and the treasuries and fought the Company's forces.

Causes: The 1770 Bengal famine and harsh British economic policies.

Leaders: Majnum Shah, Chirag Ali, Musa Shah, Bhawani Pathak, Debi Chaudharani.

➤ Revolt of Moamarias (1769-99) [Assam]

Moamarias were **low-caste peasants** who followed the teachings of Aniruddhadeva, rose up **against the Ahom Kings** of Assam, and weakened their hold on power. The Moamarias made Bhatiapar their headquarters.

➤ Poligars's Revolt (1795–1805) [Tamil Nadu]

The **Poligars revolted** when the Nawab of Arcot gave the management and control of Tinneveli and the Carnatic Provinces to the **East India Company.**

This led to resentment among the poligars who had, for long, considered themselves independent sovereign authorities within their respective territories.

The cause was the deprivation of their right to collect the kaval fees. (Kaval or 'watch' was a hereditary village police office in Tamil Nadu).

➤ Paika Rebellion (1817) [Odisha]

Paikas were the hereditary traditional landed militia (foot soldiers) of Odisha who rendered martial services and policing functions in return for rent-free land (Nishkar Jagirs). It was also known as the **Khurda Rebellion.** Walter Ewer Commission recommended that the rent-free lands of Paikas be taken over by the British. This led to Paikas taking up arms in support of zamindars and peasants.

Rise in the **price of salt, abolition of Cowrie currency**, payment of taxes in silver, and extortionist land revenue policies.

Leaders: Bakshi Jagabandhu Bidyadhar, Mukunda Deva, and Dinabandhu Santra.

Used Guerrilla Warfare to fight the British - The rebellion was brutally repressed by 1818.

➤ Ahom Revolt (1828)[Assam]

The British did not withdraw from Assam after the **First Burma War (1824-26)** and tried to incorporate Ahom territories, causing resentment among people, which led to a rebellion.

The Britishers followed a conciliatory policy, and upper Assam was handed over to Maharaja Purandar Singh (Ahom King).

Leaders: Gomdhar Konwar (Ahom Prince), Maharaja Purandhar Singh, Narendra Gadadhar Singh, among others.

➤ Wahabi Movement (1830–61) [Bihar, Bengal, North West Frontier Province, Punjab]

It was an **Islamist revivalist** movement that advocated **complete adherence to Sharia.** This movement was **led by Syed Ahmed of Rai Bareilly,** who was inspired by the teachings of Abdul Wahab (Saudi Arabia) and Shah Walilullah (Delhi). Titu Mir led the movement in the Bengal region.

Syed Ahmed condemned the Western influence on Islam and advocated a return to pure Islam and society. **Sithana and Patna** were important centers, with missions across Hyderabad, Madras, Bengal, the United Provinces, and Bombay.

➤ Kuka Movement (1840–72) [Punjab]

The Kuka Movement was founded in **1840 by Bhagat Jawahar Mal** (also called Sian Saheb) in western Punjab as a Socio-religious movement working against caste discrimination, promoting intermarriages, widow remarriages etc.

After the British took Punjab, the movement transformed from a religious purification campaign to a political campaign.

Baba Ram Singh, founder of the **Namdhari Sect** and a major leader of the movement, was deported to Rangoon in 1872.

➤ Revolt of Kerala Varma Pazhassi Raja (1797-1805) [Kerala]

Kerala Varma Pazhassi Raja, also known as the "Kerala Simham" or 'Pyche raja, was the de facto head of **Kottayam in the Malabar region.**

The Third Anglo-Mysore War resulted in British control over Kottayam.

The British appointed Vira Varma as the Raja, who imposed exorbitant taxes, leading to mass peasant resistance, led by Pyche Raja in 1793.

➤ Revolt of Diwan Velu Thampi (1808–09) [Travancore]

Harsh conditions in **Travancore** following a **subsidiary alliance agreement (1805) with Wellesley** led to resentment in the region.

The high-handed attitude of the Company led Prime Minister Velu Thampi to rebel against them, with support from Nair troops.

He openly called for armed resistance against the British in the Kundara Proclamation, sparking widespread rebellion.

A large-scale military operation was necessary to restore peace as the Maharaja of Travancore defected to the Company's side.

Important Peasant Movements

➤ Narkelberia Uprising (1782-1831) [Bengal]

Mir Nithar Ali, also known as **Titu Mir**, inspired the Muslim tenants to rise against landlords, (primarily Hindu, who imposed a beard tax on the Faraizis), and **British indigo planters.**

It is often considered the first armed peasant uprising against the British.

The revolt evolved into a religious conflict and merged into the Wahabi Movement.

➤ Pagal Panthis (1825-1835) [North East India]

It was a semi-religious group in the Mymensingh district, primarily consisting of the **Hajong and Garo tribes. Karam Shah** founded it.

Tribal peasants, led by **Karam Shah's son Tipu,** organised to resist zamindar oppression. They refused to pay rent beyond a specified limit and actively attacked the houses of zamindars.

The government introduced an equitable arrangement to protect the rights of the tribal peasants, but it was violently suppressed.

➢ Moplah Uprisings (1836-1854)

Twenty-two rebellions took place during these years. Causes included high revenue demand, reduction of field size, and oppression by British officials. **Note:** The Second Moplah uprising occurred in 1921.

Important Tribal Revolts

➢ Pahariyas Rebellion (1778) [Raj Mahal Hills]

The Pahariyas, hill dwellers near Rajmahal hills, subsisted through forest produce and shifting cultivation, maintaining independence due to geographical isolation.

Conflict escalated in the late 18th century with British-promoted settled agriculture, leading to intensified Pahariya raids. In the 1770s, the British violently attacked Pahariyas, prompting a rebellion in 1778 led by **Raja Jagganath.** In the 1780s, British pacification included annual allowances to Paharia chiefs for ensuring proper conduct.

➢ Revolt of Tilka Manjhi [Santhal Pargana]

Tilka Majhi (Jabra Paharia), led a revolt in the Pargana against British policies, particularly opposing the divide-and-rule strategy.

Operating around Sultanganj, Tilka targeted East India Company boats along the Ganga, looting the British treasury and sharing the spoils with the poor.

He organized **guerrilla warfare,** also involving **Santhal women.** In 1778, Tilka, along with Paharia Sardars, captured the Ramgarh Camp, and in 1784, he led an attack on Bhagalpur, allegedly shooting the British magistrate Augustus Cleveland.

➢ Jungle Mahal Revolt or Chuar Uprisings (1776) [Chota Nagpur]

The initial rebellion erupted in response to a hike in revenue imposed on jungle zamindars, aggravated by British instructions to demolish mud forts in 1767. Between Chota Nagpur and the plains of Bengal (Parganas in Birbhum, Bankura, and Midnapore).

In 1768, Ghatsila's zamindar, **Jagannath Singh**, and thousands of Chuar followers rebelled, leading to the capitulation of the Company government. In 1771, Chuar sardars Shyam Ganjan, Subla Singh, and Dubraj rose in rebellion, but it was subsequently suppressed.

The most significant Chuar uprising occurred in 1798 under **Durjan Singh**, prompted by discontent with East India Company policies, including the Permanent Settlement and changes in police regulations.

➢ Santhal Rebellion (1855-56) [Bihar]

Santhals moved into the Rajmahal area in the late 1770s and early 1780s to live a settled life. **Santhal and Paharia feud** (It has been called a battle between the hoe and the plough: the hoe symbolising the Paharias who used the tool in shifting cultivation and the plough standing for the Santhals who used it for settled agriculture) was settled by the formation of Daman-i-Koh (a Persian term meaning outside edges of the hills). A portion of land at the foothills was declared to be that of the Santhals.

The taxes levied by the Company government under the Permanent Settlement Act of 1793 on their land were heavy and money had to be borrowed to pay off debts. But the diku (outsiders) moneylenders charged very high rates of interest and, when debts remained unpaid, took possession of the land. Slowly, zamindars were taking over the Damin tracts.

The rebellion soon turned into a movement against the British colonial state. The Santhals called the rebellion 'hul', meaning a movement for liberation.

Led by Sidhu and Kanhu Murmu to end Company Rule and carve out an autonomous territory. Post the revolt, Santhal Pargana was created out of the districts of Bhagalpur and Birbhum with special laws for tribals

➢ Birsa Munda Revolt (1890s-1901) [Singhbhum & Ranchi]

Also known as **'The Ulgulan' (Great Tumult)**. The aim was to establish an independent Munda Raj with religious and political independence.

The British introduction of the zamindari system led to the imposition of rent on tribal land, causing eviction for non-payment and increased dependence on usurious moneylenders. So, the movement started with anger against moneylenders and outsiders ('dikus'), including Christian Missionaries.

Later, the Government took measures like the abolishment of compulsory begar, and passage of the Tenancy Act of 1903, which recognised Mundas' Khuntkatti system. The Chotanagpur Tenancy Act was passed in 1908.

4.4: The Revolt of 1857

The 19th Native Infantry at Berhampore (West Bengal) refused to use the newly introduced Enfield rifle and broke out in mutiny in February 1857, It was disbanded in March 1857.

Mangal Pande of 34th Native Infantry fired at the sergeant major of his unit at **Barrackpore.**

He was overpowered and executed. His regiment was disbanded.

CAUSES

Racism and the superiority complex of Britishers led to fissures, as seen in the lack of promotions and privileges to native soldiers and the lack of foreign service allowance in areas like Sindh, and Punjab.

General Service Enlistment Act (1856): It decreed that all future recruits to the Bengal Army would have to give an undertaking to serve anywhere. This meant that recruits had to cross the sea, and crossing the sea in Hindu belief, meant loss of caste.

➢ **Economic**

The Peasants were heavily taxed. They had to take loans from moneylenders at usurious rates. They later faced evictions due to non-payment of debt, leading to landlessness.

The Artisans lost patronage because native rulers and nobles came under economic duress. The **Zamindars lost** their lands due to the frequent use of a quo warranto by the administration.

British Industrial policy discouraged Indian handicrafts (high tariff duties) as well as thedevelopment of modern industries (no permits were given).

➢ **Political.**

British Expansionary Policies like "Subsidiary Alliance", "Doctrine of Lapse", and "Effective Control" created dependence of native rulers on the British.

Awadh Annexation (1856): Popular Nawab Wajid Ali Shah was displaced.

➢ **Administrative.**

Corruption was rampant, especially at lower levels in courts, police and land records.

The character of the British rule imparted a foreign and alien look in the eyes of Indians, giving a feeling of absentee sovereignty.

➢ **Socio-Religious**

Christian missionaries were seen with suspicion by the locals.

Socio-religious reforms like Sati Abolition and Widow remarriage were seen as unnecessary interference in religious matters by the British.

Rumours of mixing of bone dust in atta (flour), grease of cartridges being made of beef (angered Hindus) and pig fat (angered Muslims) enraged the religio-cultural sensibilities of the Sepoys.

Major Centres	Leader
Delhi	Bahadur Shah Zafar, the last Mughal King. General Bakht Khan, a zamindar.
Lucknow	Begum Hazrat Mahal proclaimed her minor son Birjis Qadir as Nawab
Faizabad	Maulvi Ahmadullah
Kanpur	Nana Saheb, the adopted son of Baji Rao II, proclaimed himself Peshwa
Jhansi and Gwalior	Rani Laxmibai (Supported by Tantia Tope, an associate of Nana Saheb)
Bareilly	Khan Bahadur
Bihar	Kunwar Singh

Causes of Failure of Revolt and Significance

The eastern, southern, and western parts of India remained more or less unaffected.

Most Indian rulers remained **loyal to the British,** such as **Scindia of Gwalior, and Holkar of Indore.**

o Big zamindars and moneylenders stayed away as they felt their interests were best served under the British.

o The feudal, conservative nature of the revolt alienated the educated middle class.

Poor quality of weapons used did not stand a chance against British weaponry

Uncoordinated nature of attacks against exceptional warfare abilities of military commanders like James Outram and Henry Havelock.

No unified ideology or future vision to bind the mutineers.

Consequences of the Revolt

➢ Enactment of Act of Better Government of India, 1858

○ Abolition of company rule.

○ Queen Victoria was declared as sovereign of British India.

○ Appointment of Secretary of State to take direct administrative control away from East India Company.

➢ Queen's Proclamation of 1858.

○ Made Lord Canning (Governor General of India) take the title of 'Viceroy'.

○ People of India promised freedom of religion, equality of all and non-interference by the British in personal affairs.

➢ Re-organisation of the army done under the "Divide and Rule" philosophy of the British

○ Caste/Community/Region became the basis of new army units

○ 'Martial races' doctrine rewarded loyalty during the rebellion and increased recruitment from Punjab, Nepal and the North-western frontier region.

○ Army Amalgamation Scheme, 1861: Moved Company's European troops to services of the crown.

○ The British stopped its socio-cultural reformist zeal, deemed as the **"White Man's Burden"**, and shifted to non-interference in matters of Indian society.

4.5: Socio-Religious Reform Movements

➢ Raja Ram Mohan Roy (1772-1833)

• He was often called the father of the Indian Renaissance.

• He called for a reduction of export duties on Indian goods abroad and the abolition of the East India Company's trading rights.

• He demanded the Indianization of superior services and the separation of the executive from the judiciary.

• He authored "Gift to Monotheists" (1809) and **translated Vedas** to advocate for monotheism within Hinduism.

• He set up **Atmiya Sabha** in **1814 (society of friends)**, aimed to propagate monotheistic ideals of Vedanta.

• **Brahmo Sabha**, founded in **1828** and later renamed Brahmo Samaj, emphasized the worship of the eternal being via prayers, meditation, and Upanishad readings, explicitly excluding any form of imagery to oppose idolatry and rituals.

• It denounced polytheism, idolatry, faith in avatars, the paramount stature of any one scripture, and the caste system.

• Anti-sati campaign began in 1818, leading to the government regulation in 1829, declaring sati a crime.

➤ Later Brahmo Samaj

• **Debendranath Tagore** joined the Brahmo Samaj in 1842. He headed the <u>**Tattvabodhini Sabha (founded in 1839)**</u>, which, along with its organ Tattvabodhini Patrika in Bengali.

• After the **split with Keshab Chandra Sen**, Debendranath Tagore's Samaj came to be known as the Adi Brahmo Samaj.

• **Keshab Chandra Sen expanded** Brahmo Samaj's reach beyond Bengal and later formed Brahmo Samaj of India in 1866.

• In 1878, Keshab's act of getting his 13-year-old daughter married to the minor Hindu Maharaja of Cooch-Behar with all the orthodox Hindu rituals caused **another split in Keshab's Brahmo Samaj of India.**

• Ananda Mohan Bose, Shibchandra Deb, and Umesh Chandra Datta created the Sadharan Brahmo Samaj in opposition to the ideas of Keshab Chandra Sen.

➤ Prarthana Samaj (1867)

• Keshab Chandra Sen helped <u>**Atmaram Pandurang**</u> in the foundation of Prarthana Samaj in Bombay.

• It primarily focused on social reforms rather than religious doctrines with a focus on disapproval of the caste system, women's education, widow remarriage, and raising the age of marriage for both males and females.

➤ Young Bengal Movement (Late 1820s - Early 1830s)

It was a radical intellectual movement that emerged among the youth in Bengal led by <u>**Henry Vivian Derozio, an Anglo-Indian**</u> and a teacher at Hindu College from 1826 to 1831.

The Derozians continued **Rammohan Roy's tradition** of public education on social, economic, and political issues.

Advocacy for Indian representation in higher services;
Support for ryots' protection and fair treatment of Indian labour abroad;
Calls for the revision of the Company's charter, freedom of the press, and trial by jury were some of their demands.

➤ Ishwar Chandra Vidyasagar (1850)

• He assumed the role of **principal at Sanskrit College** in **1850** and aimed to dismantle the priestly monopoly over scriptural knowledge by opening the college to non-Brahmins.

• He initiated a movement supporting **widow remarriage**, resulting in the legalisation of this practice.

• He opposed child marriage and polygamy while championing women's education.

• <u>**Bethune School**</u> began as a Hindu Female School in 1849 and was **renamed** Bethune School in 1856.

• Ishwar Chandra Vidyasagar was appointed as the secretary of Bethune School/College established in 1849.

➤ Jyotirao and Savitribai Phule

• Jyotirao Phule founded the **Satyashodhak Samaj** (Truth Seeker's Society) **in 1873**, with the leadership of the samaj coming from the backward classes.

• The main aims of the movement were (i) social service, and (ii) spread of education among women and lower caste people.

• He **introduced the term 'Dalit'** to describe the oppressed and advocated for a society free of exploitation; Satyashodhak marriage ceremonies challenged Brahminical practices.

• Phule's works, Sarvajanik Satyadharma and Gulamgiri became sources of inspiration for the common masses.

• **Received the title of Mahatma in 1888** from social reformer Vithalrao Krishnaji Vandekar.

• He along with his wife, established the Native Female School in Pune in 1863 and the Society for Promoting the Education of Mahars, Mangs, and others.

Savitribai Phule

She started Mahila Seva Mandal to raise awareness about women's rights, campaigned against the dehumanization of widows and advocated

for widow remarriage. She is said to have organised a successful barber's strike to denounce the inhumane practice of shaving widow's heads.

She, along with Jyotiba, established **<u>Balhatya Pratibandhak Griha</u>** to prevent infanticide in 1863.

➤ Swami Vivekananda (Narendranath Dutta) (1862–1902)

• **Vivekananda** was influenced by Ramakrishna Paramahamsa's spiritual experiences, Upanishads, Gita, Buddha, and Jesus. He subscribed to Vedanta, advocating it as a rational and superior approach. He emerged as a preacher of neo-Hinduism.

• His mission was to **bridge the gap** between **Paramartha (service)** and **Vyavahara (behaviour)** and between spirituality and daily life.

• Swami Vivekananda made a significant impact with his interpretations. He called for a balance between spiritualism and materialism.

• **Lectured in the USA and London** before returning to India in 1897.

• Aimed to instil pride in India's past and confidence in its future.

• Promoted the **unification of Hinduism** and the upliftment of the downtrodden.

➤ Dayananda Saraswati or Mulshanker (1824–83)

• He founded **Arya Samaj in 1875** in Bombay in response to Western influences.

• Later the headquarters was shifted to Lahore.

• His vision was outlined in his work **Satyarth Prakash** which aimed for a classless and casteless society, a united India, and freedom from foreign rule by advocating a return to Vedic principles. He gave the slogan "Back to the Vedas".

➤ Self-Respect Movement (1920s)

• E.V. Ramaswamy Naicker from the Balija Naidu caste initiated the movement in the **mid-1920s**, seeking **to reject Brahmanical religion and culture**, perceived as instruments of exploitation.

➤ Theosophical Movement

• Established in 1875 in **New York** City by **Madame H.P. Blavatsky** and **Colonel M.S. Olcott** as a movement inspired by Indian thought and culture.

• In 1882, the society relocated its headquarters to Adyar, near Madras.

• It embraced Hindu concepts such as reincarnation and karma, drawing inspiration from the Upanishads, yoga, and Vedanta. It opposed child marriage and advocated the abolition of caste discrimination, uplift of and improvement in the condition of widows.

• In **1907, Annie Besant became the President** (she came to India in 1893). Her initiatives include establishing the Central Hindu College in Benaras in 1898.

• The college became the nucleus for the formation of Benaras Hindu University in 1916.

MUSLIM REVIVALIST MOVEMENTS

➤ SIR SYED AHMED KHAN (1817-98)

• His aim was to reconcile Western scientific education with Quranic teachings and adapt religion to contemporary rationalism. However, he also held the Quran to be the final authority.

• He believed in the fundamental underlying unity of religions or 'practical morality'. He also preached the basic commonality of Hindu and Muslim interests.

• Established Mohammedan Anglo-Oriental College (Aligarh Muslim University) in 1875, advocated for women's education, and opposed purdah and polygamy.

• His ideas were propagated through his magazine Tahdhib-ul-Akhlaq (improvement of manners and morals).

➤ DEOBAND SCHOOL (1866)

• Founded at Darul Uloom in Saharanpur, it was organized by orthodox Muslim ulema with aims to propagate pure Quranic teachings and sustain the spirit of jihad by Muhammad Qasim Nanautavi (1832–80) and Rashid Ahmad Gangohi (1828–1905).

• Mahmud-ul-Hasan provided political and intellectual content. He worked out a synthesis of Islamic principles and nationalist aspirations. The Jamiat-ul-Ulema gave a concrete shape to Hasan's ideas of protection of the religious and political rights of the Muslims.

• Shibli Numani supported the inclusion of the English language and European sciences. He founded the Nadwatal Ulama and Darul Uloom in Lucknow in 1894–96.

➤ WAHABI/WALIULLAH MOVEMENT (18th Century)

• Inspired by Abdul Wahab of Arabia and Shah Walliullah (1702–63), it emerged as a revivalist reaction to Western influences and the degeneration of Indian Muslims.

• Shah Abdul Aziz and Syed Ahmad Barelvi popularized Walliullah's teachings, adding a political perspective. It has called for a return to the true spirit of Islam, it emphasized harmony among Muslim jurisprudence schools and the role of individual conscience in religious interpretations.

➤ TITU MIR'S MOVEMENT (1831)

• Syed Mir Nisar Ali, popularly known as Titu Mir, a disciple of Syed Ahmad Barelvi and an adherent follower of Wahabism, led a movement advocating Sharia principles in Bengal.

• Organizing Muslim peasants against Hindu landlords and British indigo planters, the movement, though not as militant as portrayed, witnessed a confrontation with the British police in 1831, resulting in his death.

➤ FARAIZI MOVEMENT (1819)

• Founded by Haji Shariatullah, aimed at eradicating un-Islamic practices in East Bengal.

• Led by Haji's son, Dudu Mian, the movement turned revolutionary in 1840, organizing a paramilitary force against Hindu landlords and Indigo planters.

➤ AHMADIYYA MOVEMENT (1889)

• Founded by Mirza Ghulam Ahmad, it embraced liberal principles and described itself as the standard-bearer of the Mohammedan Renaissance.

• It based itself, like the Brahmo Samaj, on the principles of the universal religion of all humanity; opposed jihad (sacred war against non-Muslims) and promoted Western liberal education.

• It believed in separating the mosque from the State, human rights, and tolerance.

4.6: Begining of Modern Nationalism in India

Political Associations Before the Indian National Congress

Bangabhasha Prakasika Sabha(1836): Formed by associates of Raja Rammohan Roy.

Zamindari Association (1837): Founder: Dwarkanath Tagore More popularly known as the 'Landholders' Society' was formed to safeguard the landlord's interest.

Bengal British India Society (1843): Founder: George Thompson, Dwarkanath Tagore, Chandra ohan Chatterjee, and Parmananda Maitra.

• Collection and dissemination of information relating to the actual condition of the people of British India

British Indian Association (1851): President: Radhakant Deb & General Secretary: Debendranath Tagore.

• Product of merger of Landholders Society and Bengal British India Society.

• It gave a petition to the British Parliament in 1852 when the new Charter Act was being discussed.

East India Association (1866): Under Dadabhai Naoroji in London for discussion of Indian issues and influencing English public figures to promote Indian welfare and later established branches in major Indian cities.

Poona Sarvajanik Sabha(1867): By Mahadev Govind Ranade and others as a liaison between the government and the people.

Indian Association of Calcutta (Indian National Association) (1876): Led by Surendranath Banerjea and Ananda Mohan Bose for discontent with conservative and pro-landlord policies of the British Indian Association

• Against age reduction in ICS examination (1877) and demanded simultaneous holding of civil service examinations in England and India and Indianisation of higher administrative posts.

• Campaign against the Repressive Arms Act and the Vernacular Press Act.

All-India Conference (1883): Sponsored by the Indian Association of Calcutta.

• Hosted a significant conference in Calcutta from December 28 to 30, laying the groundwork for an all-India nationalist organization. In 1886, it merged with the INC.

Madras Mahajan Sabha (1884): Established by M. Viraraghavachari (also, Veeraraghavachariar), B. Subramania Aiyer, and P. Anandacharlu.

Bombay Presidency Association (1885): Initiated by Badruddin Tyabji, Pherozeshah Mehta, and K.T. Telang.

4.7: India National Congress

A.O. Hume, a retired English civil servant, played a crucial role in shaping an all-India organization.

He collaborated with leading intellectuals of the time to organize the first session of the INC.

First Congress Session

• Held: At Gokuldas Tejpal Sanskrit College in Bombay in December 1885.

It was attended by 72 delegates, mostly lawyers.
Contemporary British Viceroy: Lord Dufferin.

Year	Place	President	Remarks
1885	Bombay	WC Banerjee	First Congress President.
1886	Calcutta	Dadabhai Naoroji	Presided over INC three times (in 1886,1893 and 1906.)
1887	Madras	Badruddin Taiyabji	1st Muslim INC President.
1888	Allahabad	George Yule	1st Englishman to become INC President.
1917	Calcutta	Annie Basent	1st Women President of INC (1917).
1924	Belagram	Mahatma Gandhi	Presided over only one session.

• Other notable figures who served as Presidents in the early years of the Congress included Pherozeshah Mehta, P. Anandacharlu, Surendranath Banerjee, Romesh Chandra Dutt, Ananda Mohan Bose, and Gopal Krishna Gokhale.

• In 1890, **Kadambini Ganguly**, the **first woman graduate** of Calcutta University, addressed the Congress session.

Madan Mohan Malviya

• He presided over the INC the maximum number of times, 4 times (1909, 1918, 1930 and 1932).
• Mahatma Gandhi regarded him as "the maker of modern India".

Moderate Phase

- **<u>Important Leders:</u>** Dadabhai Naoroji,Pherozeshah Mehta,D.E. Wacha, S.N. Banerjea, W.C. Bonnerjee.
- **<u>3P method:</u>** Petition, Prayer, and Propaganda.
- They believed that the British wanted to be just to the Indians but were not aware of the real conditions. Believed in Liberalism and constitutional agitation within legal boundaries.
- They advocated for an independent Indian economy, reduced land revenue, better working conditions, and protection of local industries.
- Their **demands were partially addressed in the Indian Councils Act of 1892,** which expanded councils but did not meet nationalist desires for more power.
- **Emphasis on constitutional methods**, economic critique, and demands for greater Indian participation in governance played a significant role in shaping the early nationalist movement in India. Their social base was narrow.

Extremist Phase (1905-18)

Factors for the Rise of Extremism

- Moderate writings exposed the real character of Britishers.
- Growth of Confidence and Self-Respect
- Growth of Education
- International Influences
- Existence of a Militant School of Thought
- Conservative Policies of Lord Curzon

The Swadeshi and Boycott Movement (1903–1905)

- The Swadeshi Movement originated **in response to the British decision to partition Bengal**, officially announced in December 1903.
- While the official reason was administrative efficiency, the actual motive was perceived to be the British desire to weaken Bengal, a center of Indian nationalism. The partition aimed to divide Bengalis based on language and religion.
- Used methods like petitions, public meetings, and newspapers such as Hitabadi, Sanjibani, and Bengalee to oppose the partition.
- The **Boycott Resolution** was passed on **August 7, 1905**, marking the formal proclamation of the Swadeshi Movement.
- A large number of students and women participated for the first time.

• In **August 1906 National Council of Education** was established to orient education on nationalist lines.

• **Satishchandra Mukherjee** pioneered the national education movement by founding the **Bhagabat Chatuspathi in 1895**. His newspaper Dawn (1897), and his Dawn Society, were set up in 1902.

• **Bengal National College** was established with **Aurobindo Ghosh** as its principal, and its **first president was Rashbehari Ghosh.**

• During the Swadeshi Movement, **Rabindranath Tagore founded Shantiniketan.**

• In the economic field, **indigenous enterprises** like the **Bengal Chemicals** factory by **Praful Chandra Ray** and, the **Swadeshi steam navigation** company by **Chidambaram Pillai.**

• Encouraged indigenous enterprises like textile mills, soap factories, tanneries, banks, and shops to promote Indian products and self-reliance.

• **Sakharam Ganesh Deuskar** published **Desher Katha in 1904**. The work inspired the Swadeshi activists. It was the inspiration for many Swadeshi street plays and folk songs, besides becoming mandatory reading for the Swadeshi activists. He popularized the ideas of **Dadabhai Naoroji and Mahadev Govind Ranade** and promoted Swadeshi in a popular idiom. Warned against the colonial state's "hypnotic conquest of the mind".

• A Number of Samitis, like Swadesh Bandab Samiti by Ashwini Kumar Dutt, came into existence.

• **Abanindranath Tagore** broke the domination of Victorian naturalism over the Indian art scene and took inspiration from Ajanta, Mughal, and Rajput paintings. Nandalal Bose was the first recipient of a scholarship offered by the Indian Society of Oriental Art, founded in 1907.

Surat Split

The Congress split into a Moderate-Extremist faction at **Surat in December 1907.**

The session was presided over by RasBehari Ghosh.

• Extremists aimed for the Nagpur session with Tilak or Lajpat Rai as President and reiteration of radical resolutions. Moderates wanted the Surat session to exclude Tilak from the presidency, seeking to drop radical resolutions.

- Congress was dominated by Moderates post-split, reiterating commitment to self-government within the British Empire through constitutional methods.

<u>**Government Repression:**</u> The government enacted stringent laws (1907-1911) to curb anti-government activities, such as the Seditious Meetings Act (1907), Criminal Law Amendment Act (1908), Incitement to Offences Act (1908), Explosive Substances Act (1908), and Indian Press Act (1910).

Delhi Durbar

- In **1911, Lord Hardinge** organized a Durbar in Delhi, which was attended by the British Monarch King George V and Queen Mary.
- Announcements in Delhi Durbar - **Bengal Partition was revoked**.
- **British India's capital shifted** from Calcutta to Delhi.
- **Delhi Conspiracy Case:** Rash Bihari Bose and Sachindran Sanyal, extremist revolutionaries tried to throw a bomb on Hardinge.
  - **Sachindran Sanyal** was jailed during which he wrote Bandi Jeevan.

4.8: The Surge of Revolutionary Activities in India

BENGAL

<u>**1902:**</u> Anushilan Samiti was founded by Promotha Mitter, Jatindranath Banerjee, Barindra Kumar Ghosh and others.

<u>**1906:**</u> Inner Circle within Anushilan (Barindra Kumar Ghosh, Bhupendranath Dutta) launched the weekly Yugantar newspaper.

<u>**1907:**</u> Rashbehari Bose and Sachin Sanyal organized a secret society covering Punjab, Delhi, and the United Provinces. Hemachandra Kanungo went abroad for military and political training.

<u>**1907 – 1908:**</u>

- Prafulla Chaki and Khudiram Bose attempted to bomb a carriage supposed to be carrying Judge Kingsford in Muzaffarpur, resulting in the unintended death of two British ladies and
- Trial of Anushilan group members, including Aurobindo and Barindra Ghosh, took place in the Alipore conspiracy case (Manicktolla bomb conspiracy or Muraripukur conspiracy).

• Narendra Gosain (or Goswami), who had turned approver and Crown witness, was shot dead by two co-accused, Satyendranath Bose and Kanailal Dutta, in jail.

Dec 1912: Rashbehari Bose and Sachin Sanyal staged a bomb attack on Viceroy Hardinge during his official entry into Delhi, injuring him. Investigations led to the Delhi Conspiracy trial.

During World War I

Jugantar party, led by Bagha Jatin (Jatindranath Mukherjee), planned the 'German Plot' or 'Zimmerman Plan' to import German arms, aimed at an all-India insurrection.

MAHARASHTRA

1879: Vasudev Balwant Phadke organized the Ramosi Peasant Force, aiming to trigger an armed revolt against the British by disrupting communication lines among others.

1890: Bal Gangadhar Tilak propagated militant nationalism, advocating violence, during Ganapati and Shivaji festivals and through his journals Kesari and Maharatta.

1897: Tilak's disciples, the Chapekar brothers (Damodar and Balkrishna), assassinated the Plague Commissioner of Poona, Rand, and Lieutenant Ayerst.

1899: Savarkar and his brother organized the **Mitra Mela**, a secret society, which later merged with **Abhinav Bharat** (inspired by Mazzini's 'Young Italy') in 1904 and Centres of bomb manufacture emerged in Nasik, Poona, sand Bombay.

1909: A.M.T. Jackson, the Collector of Nasik, was assassinated by Anant Lakshman Kanhere, a member of Abhinav Bharat. The assassination was part of a larger conspiracy aiming to overthrow the British government through armed revolution. Thirty-eight people were arrested, whereas Savarkar was identified as the brain and leader of the conspiracy, and was sentenced to transportation for life and the forfeiture of all his property.

PUNJAB

• **Lala Lajpat Rai:** Published Punjabee with the motto of self-help at any cost.

• **Ajit Singh:** Organized the extremist Anjuman-i-Mohisban-i-Watan in Lahore, and published Bharat Mata. He was Bhagat Singh's uncle.

• Other influential leaders included Aga Haidar, Syed Haider Raza, Bhai Parmanand, and the radical Urdu poet, Lalchand 'Falak'.

Revolutionary Activities Abroad

• **1905:** Shyamji Krishnavarma started **India House (London)**, a center for Indian students, offering scholarships to radical youth from India. The Indian Sociologist journal was published here.

• **Madanlal Dhingra**, associated with India House, assassinated Curzon-Wyllie, a bureaucrat, in London in 1909.

• In **1910, Savarkar** was extradited and transported for life in the Nasik conspiracy case, making London unsafe for revolutionaries.

• Paris and Geneva emerged, where **Madam Bhikaji Cama** brought out Bande Mataram and **Ajit Singh** operated.

• **1909:** After the deterioration of Anglo-German Relations, Virendranath Chattopadhyaya made Berlin his base.

• **1911:** It had been carried on by Ramdas Puri, G.D. Kumar, Taraknath Das, Sohan Singh Bhakna, and Lala Hardayal set up a 'Swadesh Sevak Home' at Vancouver and 'United India House' at Seattle.

• **Ghadr Party:** Established in San Francisco in 1913 with branches along the US coast and in the Far East. Its leaders include - Lala Hardayal, Ramchandra, Bhagwan Singh, Kartar Singh Saraba, Barkatullah, and Bhai Parmanand.

• Objectives: Organize assassinations, publish anti-imperialist literature, work among Indian troops abroad, procure arms, and incite a simultaneous revolt in British colonies.

• **Rashbehari Bose:** He was a leading figure in the Ghadr Revolution during World War I. [UPSC 2022]

• **1913:** Rashbehari Bose met Jatin to discuss the possibility of an all-India armed uprising akin to the 1857 revolt. He collaborated with Bagha Jatin, extending the Bengal plan to Punjab and the upper provinces. The revolution plan didn't succeed, prompting Rashbehari Bose's escape to Japan in 1915.

He later played a significant role in founding the Indian National Army.

Komagata Maru Incident

• 1914: Komagata Maru, a ship carrying mainly Sikh and Punjabi Muslim immigrants, was turned back by Canadian authorities, creating tensions. The ship later anchored at Calcutta. Inmates refused to board the Punjab-bound train. In the ensuing conflict with the police at Budge near Calcutta, 22 persons died.

• Result: The incident heightened tensions, leading Ghadr leaders to plan a violent attack to oust British rule in India.

• **1915:** The **Berlin Committee** for Indian Independence was established by Virendranath Chattopadhyay, Bhupendranath Dutta, Lala Hardayal, and others with the help of the German foreign office under 'The Zimmerman Plan'. It aimed to mobilize Indian settlers abroad, incite rebellion among Indian troops, and organize an armed invasion of British India.

4.9: WW-1 & Nationalist Response

• **Moderates** supported the **British Empire** in the **war** as a duty.

• **Extremists like Tilak** supported the **war**, hoping **for self-government as a reward for India's loyalty.**

• **Revolutionaries** saw an **opportunity to wage war** against British rule and aimed for immediate independence.

• The war drained India of troops, reducing the number of white soldiers to a mere 15,000 at one point. It raised the possibility of financial and military help from Germany and Turkey.

Home Rule Movement

• It was fueled by various socio-political factors arising from dissatisfaction with **British rule** and the **impact of World War I.**

• It aimed for Self-government or home rule for India within the British Commonwealth.

• It was **inspired by the Irish Home Rule League**, seeking autonomy similar to that demanded for Ireland.

Approach

• Public meetings, Establishment of libraries and reading rooms with political literature, Conferences and classes for students on politics.

• Propaganda through newspapers, pamphlets, posters, illustrated postcards, plays, and religious songs, Fundraising activities also social work and participation in local government activities.

• **Bal Gangadhar Tilak** and **Annie Besant** were prominent leaders. [UPSC 2013]

• **Other leaders** included G.S. Khaparde, Joseph Baptista, Muhammad Ali Jinnah, Motilal Nehru, Jawaharlal Nehru, Bhulabhai Desai, Chittaranjan Das, K.M. Munshi, B. Chakravarti, Saifuddin Kitchlew, Madan Mohan Malaviya, Tej Bahadur Sapru, Lala Lajpat Rai and Sir S. Subramania Iyer (he renounced his knighthood).

Tilak's Indian Home Rule League	Annie Besant's All-India Home Rule
Establishment: April 1916. ○ Tilak held his first Home Rule meeting at Belgaum. ○ Poona was the headquarters of his league. **Coverage:** Restricted to Maharashtra (excluding Bombay city), Karnataka, Central Provinces, and Berar with six branches. **Demands:** Swarajya (self-rule), Formation of linguistic states and Vernacular education.	Inspired by the Irish Home Rule Leagues. • **Establishment:** September 1916 in Madras (now Chennai). • **Coverage:** Covered the rest of India, including Bombay City with 200 branches. • **Key Figures:** ○ George Arundale: Organizing secretary. ○ B.W. Wadia and C.P. Ramaswamy Aiyar: Played significant roles in the league.

Lucknow Session of the Indian National Congress (1916)

President: Ambika Charan Majumdar (a Moderate leader).

Readmission of Extremists to Congress was a key aspect of this session.

Lucknow Pact - Congress and the Muslim League presented common demands to the government marking a significant unity between the two major political parties in India.

Reasons for the Change in the League's Attitude

• British Actions Leading to Discontent Among Muslims: Refusal to aid Turkey in its war, annulment of the partition of Bengal in 1911, and Refusal to establish a university at Aligarh with nationwide affiliations.

• The shift in League's Political Outlook: Younger League members leaning towards bolder nationalist politics beyond the limited scope of the Aligarh school and Calcutta session of the Muslim League in 1912 committed to working for self-government similar to Congress's goals.

4.10: Gandhiji, NCM and Khilafat Issue

Gandhiji in South Africa

• He **went to South Africa in 1893** for a legal case involving a client, Dada Abdullah.

• He established the **Natal Indian Congress** and started the **newspaper Indian Opinion.**

• The **first satyagraha** was against a law requiring Indians to carry registration certificates with fingerprints.

• **Tolstoy Farm**, founded in **1910**, was named after the Russian writer Tolstoy, admired by Gandhi.

• The second farm of its kind, with the **first being Phoenix Farm in 1904**, was inspired by John Ruskin's critique of capitalism.

Gandhi in India

• Gandhi returned to **India in January 1915.**

• Toured the country for a year to understand the condition of the masses and refrained from taking any political position initially.

➤ **Champaran Satyagraha (1917): First Civil Disobedience**

• Issue: **Indigo planters** exploiting farmers in Champaran, Bihar.

• Gandhi was requested by Rajkumar Shukla and later joined by Rajendra Prasad, Mazharul-Haq, Mahadev Desai, Narhari Parekh, and J.B. Kripalani.

• Resistance: Gandhi defied orders to leave and faced punishment.

• Outcome: Tinkathia system (Indigo to be grown on 3/20 parts of land) was abolished, peasants were compensated, first victory of civil disobedience in India.

➤ **Ahmedabad Mill Strike (February 1918): First Hunger Strike**

• Dispute: Cotton mill owners vs. workers over plague bonus.

• Gandhi got a letter from Anusuya Sarabhai, sister of Ambalal Sarabhai (mill owner and the president of the Ahmedabad Mill Owners Association) for help in fighting for justice.

- **Intervention:** Gandhi mediated, advised a non-violent strike and undertook a hunger strike.
- **Outcome:** The tribunal settled, and workers were awarded a 35% wage hike.

Kheda Satyagraha (March 1918):

First Non - Co-operation movement

Issue: Tax refusal due to crop failure and drought in Kheda, Gujarat.

Leadership: Sardar Patel and Gandhians led the tax revolt.

Unity: Communities supported the revolt, maintaining discipline.

Outcome: The government agreed to suspend taxes, reduce the rate increase, and return confiscated property.

Rowlatt Satyagraha - First Mass Strike - (April 6, 1919)

Gandhi's Response: Called the Rowlatt Act the "Black Act," urged mass protest. Peasants, artisans, & urban poor became active in struggle.

- **Forms of Protest:** Nationwide hartal (strike), fasting, prayer, civil disobedience, and courting arrest.

All the elected Indian members, including Muhammed Ali Jinnah, Madan Mohan Malaviya, and Mazhar Ul Haq, resigned in protest.

Jallianwala Bagh Massacre (April 13, 1919)

- Amritsar was worst affected by violence, showing displeasure through shop closures. Arrests of nationalist leaders Saifuddin Kitchlew and Dr Satyapal led to further protests.
- Brigadier-General **Reginald Dyer** imposed martial law to restore order - Forbade gatherings, demonstrations, and assemblies; imposed restrictions.
- **Incident:** Troops surrounded Jallianwala Bagh, and fired on an unarmed crowd without warning, causing casualties (Congress estimated over 1,000 dead, 1,500 injured).
- In response came the Hunter Committee's Report (March 1920)
  o Did not impose any penal or disciplinary action but only condemned Dyer for lack of notice to disperse before firing, he was held for overstepping authority.

Non-Cooperation Movement and Khilafat Issue

In early **1919**, leaders like the **Ali brothers** (Shaukat Ali and Muhammad Ali), **Maulana Azad, Ajmal Khan**, and **Hasrat Mohani** urged the British government to change its stance towards Turkey.

• Khalifa's control over Muslim sacred places should remain intact, and the Khalifa should retain sufficient territories after territorial arrangements.

• **Mahatma Gandhi**, as the <u>president</u> of the **All India Khilafat Committee**, saw the issue as a platform for a united (Hindu plus Muslim) mass non-cooperation movement against the British.

<u>February 1920:</u> Gandhi announces readiness for non-cooperation movement if the terms of the peace treaty fail to satisfy Indian Muslims.

<u>August 31, 1920:</u> The Khilafat Committee initiates a campaign of non-cooperation, formally launching the movement.

<u>September 1920:</u> Congress (at a special session in Calcutta) approves a non-cooperation program until Punjab and Khilafat issues are resolved, including boycotts of schools, law courts, legislative councils, foreign goods, and government titles.

Chauri Chaura Incident (February 5, 1922)

• Took place in <u>**Chauri-Chaura, Gorakhpur district**</u>, United Provinces (now Uttar Pradesh).

• Police beat a leader of volunteers protesting against liquor sale and high food prices. The police subsequently fired on the protesting crowd near the police station.

• The agitated crowd retaliated by attacking and setting fire to the police station. Twenty-two policemen died in the violence, some trying to flee but being killed and thrown back into the fire.

• Gandhi, disheartened by the increasing violence associated with the movement, immediately announced the withdrawal of the non-cooperation movement.

4.11: Emergence of Swarajists, Socialist Ideas and Revolutionary Activities

Congress-Khilafat Swarajya Party or Swarajist Party

• The differences over the question of council entry between the two schools of thought resulted in the defeat of the Swarajists' proposal of 'ending or mending' the councils at the **Gaya session** of the <u>Congress (December 1922).</u>

• **C.R. Das** and **Motilal Nehru** resigned from the presidentship and secretaryship, respectively, of the Congress and announced the formation of **Congress-Khilafat Swarajya Party** or simply **Swarajist Party**, with C.R. Das as the president and Motilal Nehru as one of the secretaries.

➤ Punjab-UP-Bihar

• Dominated by Hindustan Republican Association/Army (HRA).

• HRA was formed in October 1924 in Kanpur by leaders like Ramprasad Bismil, Jogesh Chandra Chatterjee, and Sachin Sanyal.

Kakori Robbery (August 1925)

Action of HRA, men held up the 8-Down train at Kakori, and looted its official railway cash, leading to arrests of many. **Bismil, Ashfaqullah**, Roshan Singh, and Rajendra Lahiri were hanged.

Saunders' Murder (Lahore, December 1928)

• Occurred following the **death of Lala Lajpat Rai** due to lathi blows during an anti-Simon Commission protest in October 1928.

○ HSRA revolutionaries, including Bhagat Singh, Shivram Rajguru, and Chandrashekhar Azad, sought retribution for Lajpat Rai's death.

○ **Bhagat Singh and Rajguru** mistook John P. Saunders for Superintendent of Police James Scott.

○ He shot an Indian constable while aiding Bhagat Singh and Rajguru's escape.

Bomb in the Central Legislative Assembly (April 1929)

• Protest against the Public Safety Bill and Trade Disputes Bill (restricting civil liberties)

• In HSRA leadership, **Bhagat Singh and Batukeshwar Dutt** carried out the bombing.

• Not to inflict damage but to gain attention, get arrested, and utilize the trial court as a platform for spreading their revolutionary ideology.

Bengal during the 1920s

After C.R. Das's death in **1925, the Bengal Congress split into two factions:** one led by J.M. Sengupta (supported by **Anushilan** group) and the other by Subhash Bose (backed by the **Yugantar group**).

Gopinath Saha made an attempt on the life of the infamous Calcutta Police Commissioner, Charles Tegart, in 1924. This action led to severe government reprisals, resulting in the hanging of Gopinath Saha and the arrest of many, including Subhash Bose.

• The most active and renowned among the new "Revolt Groups" was the **Chittagong group led by Surya Sen.**

Chittagong Armoury Raid (April 1930): Executed by 65 activists under the Indian Republican Army—Chittagong Branch banner, the raid proved successful. Sen hoisted the national flag, proclaimed a provisional revolutionary government, and later dispersed into nearby villages, targeting government establishments.

4.12: Simon Commission & the Nehru Report

Simon Commission was established on **November 8, 1927**, under the leadership of Sir John Simon and 7 members. The **objective** was to assess whether India was prepared for further constitutional reforms and to recommend the direction for these reforms to the British government.

Congress session in Madras under the presidency of M.A. Ansari (December 1927) decided to boycott the commission entirely.

Simon Commission Recommendations – 1930

➤ **Provincial Reforms**

• Proposed abolition of dyarchy and advocated for representative provincial governments with increased legislative council members.

• Recommended provincial autonomy with discretionary powers for the governor related to internal security and community protection.

➤ **Central Governance**

• Rejected parliamentary responsibility at the center, advocating complete power for the Governor-General in appointing cabinet members.

• Advocated the Government of India's complete control over the high court.

➤ **Communal Electorates**

• Suggested the retention and extension of separate communal electorates, though temporarily, until tensions between Hindus and Muslims subsided.

• Rejected the idea of universal franchise.

➤ **Federalism and Representation**

• It embraced the concept of federalism but proposed a gradual implementation. The suggestion involved establishing a Consultative Council of Greater India, inclusive of representatives from both British provinces and princely states.

• Recommended the establishment of local legislatures for the North-West Frontier Province and Baluchistan.

• Advocated the **separation of Sindh from Bombay** and **Burma from India**, considering them distinct from the Indian subcontinent.

• Proposed Indianizing the Indian army while retaining British forces.

NEHRU REPORT

• It was formed as **an answer to Birkenhead's challenge.**

• An All Parties Conference in February 1928 appointed a subcommittee chaired by **Motilal Nehru** to draft a constitution.

• Committee members included Tej Bahadur Sapru, Subhas Chandra Bose, M.S. Aney, Mangal Singh, Ali Imam, Shuaib Qureshi, and G.R.Pradhan. It was finalized by August 1928.

Recommendations

Dominion Status: Proposed dominion status akin to self-governing dominions, with a division among committee members—the majority favoured dominion status, while a minority sought complete independence.

Electoral System: Rejected separate electorates, and advocated joint electorates with reserved seats for minorities, not in areas where they constituted the majority (e.g., Punjab, Bengal).

Provincial Reforms: Advocated linguistic provinces.

Fundamental Rights: Proposed 19 fundamental rights, including equal rights for women, union formation, and universal adult suffrage.

Jinnah's Fourteen Points (March 1929)

• It became the basis of all future propaganda of the Muslim League

• Federal Constitution with residual powers to provinces.

• Provincial autonomy.

• No constitutional amendment by the centre without the concurrence of the states constituting the Indian federation.

• All legislatures and elected bodies to have adequate representation of Muslims in every province without reducing the majority of Muslims in a province to a minority or equality.

• Adequate representation of Muslims in the services and in self-governing bodies.

• **One-third Muslim** representation in the central legislature.

• In any cabinet at the centre or in the provinces, one-third to be Muslims.

• Separate electorates.

• No bill or resolution in any legislature is to be passed if three-fourths of a minority community considers such a bill or resolution to be against their interests.

• Any territorial redistribution not to affect the Muslim majority in Punjab, Bengal, and NWFP.

• Separation of Sindh from Bombay.

• Constitutional reforms in the NWFP and Baluchistan.

• Full religious freedom to all communities.

4.13: Civil Disobedience Movement and Round Table Conferences

Delhi Manifesto (November 2, 1929)

• It was a conference of national leaders which issued demands for attending the Round Table Conference.

• **Round Table Conference** should act as a constituent assembly to formulate a constitution for implementing Dominion status.

• **Congress** should have **majority representation** at the conference.

• General amnesty for political prisoners and a conciliatory policy were requested.

• Gandhi, Motilal Nehru, and others met Lord Irwin in December 1929;

○ Leaders sought assurance from Irwin that the Round Table Conference's purpose was to draft a constitutional scheme for Dominion status.

○ Irwin rejected the demands of the Delhi Manifesto, stating the conference's purpose was not to draft a constitutional scheme.

Lahore Congress and Purna Swaraj (December 1929)

• **Jawaharlal Nehru** became the President of the Lahore session of Congress.

• Nehru declared an open conspiracy to free the country from foreign rule and invited all countrymen to join and emphasized peaceful mass movements as essential for liberation.

Decisions at the Lahore Session

• Round Table Conference was **boycotted.**

• Declaration of **complete independence** as Congress's goal.

• Authorization was given to the **Congress Working Committee to launch civil disobedience,** including non-payment of taxes, and urged legislators to resign.

• January 26, 1930 was fixed as the first Independence (Swarajya) Day, to be celebrated everywhere.

• **December 31, 1929:** On the banks of **River Ravi, Jawaharlal Nehru hoisted the newly adopted tricolour flag** of freedom amid slogans of Inquilab Zindabad.

○ **Inquilab Zindabad,** which can be translated as "Long Live Revolution" was coined by Moulana Hasrat Mohani in the year 1921.

• Independence Pledge (Supposed to have been drafted by Gandhi)

○ Points highlighted in the pledge included the inalienable right to freedom, British exploitation, economic ruin, cultural and spiritual impact, denial of political rights, and **preparation for civil disobedience for Purna Swaraj.**

CIVIL DISOBEDIENCE MOVEMENT

The Congress Working Committee, dissatisfied with the government's lack of response to their demands, empowered Gandhi to initiate the Civil Disobedience Movement.

➤ Dandi March (March 12–April 6, 1930)

• The plan involved leading a 240-mile march with 78 members from Sabarmati Ashram through Gujarat villages. Upon reaching Dandi (a village near Surat) on the coast, they would defy the salt law by collecting salt from the beach.

• Symbolic breaking of the salt law by Gandhi at Dandi on April 6, marking the launch of the Civil Disobedience Movement.

• Civil disobedience actions included picketing foreign liquor and cloth shops, refusal to pay taxes, lawyers giving up practice, boycott of law courts, and government servants resigning.

• Nehru's arrest led to massive demonstrations in Madras, Calcutta, and Karachi.

• Gandhi's arrest came on May 4, 1930, when he led a raid on Dharasana Salt Works on the west coast.

• Consequent upon the breaking of Salt Law by Indian people, the Indian National Congress was declared illegal by the colonial rulers.

➤ Gandhi-Irwin Pact/Delhi Pact (1931)

On January 25, 1931, Gandhi and all other members of the Congress Working Committee (CWC) were released.

• It was **signed on March 5, 1931, in Delhi**, where the Viceroy was representing the British Indian Government, and Gandhi was representing the Indian people. This pact placed the Congress on an equal footing with the government.

• Immediate release of non-violent political prisoners [UPSC 2020], Remission of unpaid fines, Return of unsold lands, Lenient treatment of resigned government servants, Personal consumption salt-making rights in coastal villages, Permission for peaceful picketing, Withdrawal of emergency ordinances.

• **Rejections by Irwin**: Public enquiry into police excesses and Commutation of Bhagat Singh and comrades' death sentence.

• **Agreements by Gandhi**: Suspension of civil disobedience movement and Participation in the next Round Table Conference on constitutional matters.

➤ Karachi Congress Session (March 1931)

• It was a special session of the Congress held at Karachi to endorse the Gandhi-Irwin Pact.

• While disapproving of and dissociating itself from political violence, the Congress admired the 'bravery' and 'sacrifice' of Bhagat Singh, Sukhdev, and Rajguru.

• Reiteration of the goal of Purna Swaraj.

• Fundamental Rights Resolution was put forward.

• National Economic Programme Resolution was put forward.

The Round Table Conferences

➤ First Round Table Conference (London, November 1930 - January 1931)

• This was the first conference arranged between the British and the Indians as equals.

• Indian representation by diverse groups: Princely states, Muslim League, Hindu Mahasabha, Sikhs, Parsis, Liberals, Depressed classes, Justice party, Labour, Christians, women, universities, and others.

• The Government of India was represented by Narendra Nath Law, Bhupendra Nath Mitra, C.P. Ramaswami Iyer, and M. Ramachandra Rao.

• Outcome: Inadequate achievements; discussions on India's federation, defense and finance safeguards, transfer of departments, but little implementation, civil disobedience persisted.

➢ **Second Round Table Conference (London, September 1931 - December 1931)**

• Members of the Indian Liberal Party, such as Tej Bahadur Sapru, C.Y. Chintamani, and Srinivasa Sastri, appealed to Gandhi to talk with the Viceroy.

• The Indian National Congress nominated Gandhi as its sole representative.

• The Government of India was represented by C.P. Ramaswami Iyer, Narendra Nath Law, and M. Ramachandra Rao.

• **Issues:** Change in Viceroy from Irwin to Willingdon, Formation of a National Government in Britain and Opposition by right-wing factions in Britain against Congress's equal negotiation.

• Deadlock on minority issues; separate electorates demanded by various groups, Gandhi opposed.

• Princely states were apprehensive about federation after the suspension of the civil disobedience movement.

• **Outcome:**

○ Two Muslim-majority provinces were announced—

▪ North-West Frontier Province (NWFP) and Sindh.

○ The setting up of an Indian Consultative Committee.

○ Setting up of three expert committees—finance, franchise, and states.

○ The prospect of a unilateral British Communal Award if Indians failed to agree.

➢ **Third Round Table Conference (Nov 1932 - Dec 1932)**

• Congress and Gandhi abstained, limiting Indian leader's participation.

• Similar issues persisted, and little progress was made.

• Recommendations debated in the British Parliament, followed by the formation of a Joint Select Committee.

Government of India Act of 1935 was enforced in July 1935 based on the committee's draft Bill.

➤ Resumption of Civil Disobedience Movement (1931-1934)

On the failure of the second Round Table Conference, the Congress Working Committee decided on December 29, 1931 to resume the civil disobedience movement.

➤ Communal Award (1932)

• Announced by British PM Ramsay MacDonald on August 16, 1932.

• Based on findings of the Indian Franchise Committee (also called the Lothian Committee), it established separate electorates and reserved seats for minorities.

• Provided separate electorates for Muslims, Europeans, Sikhs, Indian Christians, Anglo-Indians, depressed classes, and Marathas in Bombay.

• Reserved seats for depressed classes amounted to 78.

• Dr. B.R. Ambedkar's Stance: Advocated the distinct treatment of depressed classes as an independent minority separate from caste Hindus.

4.14: August Offer and Cripps Mission

➤ August Offer (August 1940)

• Announced by **Lord Linlithgow** - It proposed dominion status for India and suggested **expanding the viceroy's executive council** with a majority of Indians.

• Setting up of a **constituent assembly** after the war where mainly Indians would decide the constitution according to their social, economic, and political conceptions.

• Stipulated no Constitution adoption without minority consent.

• The **National Defence Council** was established with advisory functions in 1941

Responses

• Congress rejected the August Offer.

• Nehru declared the dominion status concept as "dead as a doornail."

• Gandhi believed the offer widened the gap between nationalists and British rulers.

Muslim League welcomed the veto assurance and reiterated partition as the solution.

➤ Individual Satyagraha

• Gandhi initiated limited satyagraha individually at the end of 1940.

Objectives

○ to show that nationalist patience was not due to weakness.

○ to express Anti-War Sentiment of people making no distinction between Nazism and Indian autocracy.

○ to provide another chance for the government to peacefully accept Congress demands

• Satyagrahis demanded freedom of speech against the war through an anti-war declaration.

• If not arrested, they would repeat and then move to villages, initiating the **'Delhi Chalo Movement.'** - Vinoba Bhave and Nehru were among the first.

➤ Cripps Mission (March 1942)

Proposals

• Formation of Indian Union with dominion status.

• Convening a Constituent Assembly after a war.

• Authority of making the constitution solely to Indians for the first time, as opposed to the August offer, where it was mainly in the hands of Indians.

• Indians were allowed a significant share in the administration during the interim period.

• Blueprint for partition

4.15: Quit India Movement, Demand for Pakistan, and the INA

Due to the **Failure of the Cripps Mission**, discontent due to wartime inflation, fears of a scorched earth policy in Assam, Bengal, and Orissa against potential Japanese advancement, news of British defeats in South-East Asia, coupled with the looming threat of a British collapse, increased public readiness to express dissatisfaction.

The **Congress Working Committee** authorized **Gandhiji to lead a non-violent mass movement against the British**. This is known as the **Quit India resolution**.

• The resolution was proposed by Nehru, seconded by Sardar Patel and ratified at the Congress meeting at Gowalia Tank, Bombay, on August 8, 1942.

• **Usha Mehta** was a Gandhian and freedom fighter of India. **She organized the Congress Radio**, an underground radio station, which functioned for a few months during the Quit India Movement of 1942. To elude the authorities, the organizers moved the station's location almost daily.

➤ **Parallel Governments during Quit India Movement**

Ballia (August 1942) - Chittu Pandey - He got many Congress leaders released.

Tamluk (Dec 1942 - Sep 1944) - Midnapore - Jatiya Sarkar - Cyclone relief, school grants, supplied paddy to the poor, organised Vidyut Vahinis.

Satara (Mid-1943 - 1945) - "Prati Sarkar" - Y.B.Chavan, Nana Patil, etc. - Village libraries, Nyayadan Mandals, prohibition campaigns and 'Gandhi marriages' were organised.

➤ **Rajagopalachari Formula (1944)**

• C. **Rajagopalachari (CR)**, prepared a **formula for Congress-League cooperation.**

• It was a tacit acceptance of the League's demand for Pakistan, supported by Gandhi.

○ **Muslim League** to endorse Congress's demand for independence.

○ Cooperation in forming a provisional government at the center.

○ After the end of the war, the entire population of Muslim majority areas in North-West and North-East India to decide by a plebiscite, whether or not to form a separate sovereign state.

○ If partition is agreed upon, there should be a joint agreement to safeguard defence, commerce, and communications. The effectiveness of these terms is contingent upon England transferring full powers to India.

➤ **Desai-Liaquat Pact**

• It was an attempt to break the deadlock between Congress and the Muslim League.

• **Leaders Involved:** Bhulabhai Desai (Congress) and Liaqat Ali Khan (Muslim League).

• **Interim Government Proposal:** Equal representation from Congress and League in the central legislature for an interim government and 20% reserved seats for minorities.

• No agreement was reached on these terms. Congress and Muslim League came on parity

➤ Wavell Plan (1945) and Shimla Conference

Lord Wavell, the viceroy, was given permission to initiate negotiations with Indian leaders.

○ **Indian Majority in Executive Council:** All members, except the governor-general and commander-in-chief, to be Indians.

○ **Equal Representation** for Caste Hindus and Muslims.

○ The **reconstructed council to function as an interim** government within the 1935 Act's framework.

○ **Governor General's Veto:** Governor-general to exercise veto based on ministerial advice.

○ **Joint Party Representation:** Representatives from different parties to submit a joint or separate list for council nominations.

○ **Post-war negotiations** possibilities on a **new constitution** have been kept open.

➤ SUBHASH CHANDRA BOSE break

• Initially secured the **fourth position** in the Indian Civil Services examination **but resigned in 1921** to join the freedom struggle.

• He served as the **mayor of Calcutta in 1923**. His political guru was Chittaranjan Das.

• Bose convened an **Anti-Compromise Conference** at **Ramgarh** in March **1940**.

• It was resolved to launch a worldwide struggle on April 6, 1940, coinciding with the National Week, against imperialist war, urging people not to support the Imperialist War with resources.

• He **met Hitler** using the pseudonym Orlando Mazzotta and formed the 'Freedom Army' (Mukti Sena) with Indian prisoners of war captured by Germany and Italy.

• Dresden, Germany, became the headquarters of the Freedom Army.

• **Bose came to be called 'Netaji' by the people of Germany.**

• He gave the **famous slogan, 'Jai Hind'** from the Free India Centre, Germany.

• Started **regular broadcasts from Berlin radio** in January 1942.

• He travelled via German and Japanese submarines, to reach Japan and then Singapore by July 1943.

➢ Indian National Army (INA)

The **first division** of the **INA** was formed with **16,300 men** in **September 1942.**

• **Mohan Singh**, with the support of the Japanese, **formed the Indian National Army (INA)** by recruiting Indian prisoners of war (POWs).

• A **conference in Bangkok** decided to place the INA under the Indian Independence League, **chaired by Rashbehari Bose**.

• He founded the League in Tokyo in 1942. The Japanese sought Subhas Bose to lead the INA.

• In **July 1943, Bose met Rashbehari** Bose in Singapore, who willingly transferred control of the Indian Independence League and the INA to him.

• **Subhas Bose** became the **Supreme Commander** of the **INA** on **August 25**.

• On **October 21, 1943**, Subhas Bose formed the **Provisional Government for Free India** in **Singapore** with H.C. Chatterjee (Finance portfolio), M.A. Aiyar (Broadcasting), and Lakshmi Swaminathan (Women Department).

• The famous slogan, **"Give me blood, I will give you freedom,"** was coined in Malaya.

• A women's regiment, named **Rani Jhansi Regiment**, was formed.

• The **INA headquarters** moved **to Rangoon (Burma) in January 1944**, and the army recruits were to march with the **war cry "Chalo Delhi!".**

• On **November 6, 1943**, the Japanese army handed over the Andaman and Nicobar Islands to the INA. On **July 6, 1944**, Bose addressed Gandhi as the 'Father of the Nation' from the Azad Hind Radio, marking the first use of this term. The **Azad Hind Fauz entered Indian soil** on **March 18, 1944**, after crossing the Burma border.

• On **April 14, 1944**, Colonel Malik raised the **INA flag at Moirang, Manipur.** This marked the first hoisting of the INA flag on the Indian mainland.

• INA carried out military administration duties at Moirang for three months. Allied forces reclaimed the territory, leading to the withdrawal of INA brigades on July 18, 1944.

• On **August 18, 1945, Subhas Bose reportedly died** in a mysterious air crash in Taipei, Taiwan.

• INA POWs were brought back to India after the war for court-martial.

➤ **INA Trials**

• Public trials were held for hundreds of INA prisoners. Mass pressure against INA trials led to a decisive shift in government policy.

• The **first INA trial** took place in **November 1945 at the Red Fort** in Delhi, with Prem Kumar Sehgal, a Hindu, Shah Nawaz Khan, a Muslim, and Gurbaksh Singh Dhillon, a Sikh. This acted as a common denominator for all Indians.

• Bhulabhai Desai, Tej Bahadur Sapru, Kailash Nath Katju, Jawaharlal Nehru, and Asaf Ali organized the defence for INA prisoners in court. INA Relief and Enquiry Committee helped the affected persons.

4.16: The Cabinet Mission

The **Cabinet Mission arrived in Delhi on March 24, 1946**, and engaged in prolonged discussions with Indian leaders from all parties and groups on the issues of the interim government and the principles and procedures for framing a new constitution to grant freedom to India.

• The Congress and the League failed to reach an agreement on the fundamental issue of India's unity or partition.

• Due to this, the Cabinet Mission introduced its own plan in May 1946 to address the constitutional problem.

Key Points

• Large non-Muslim populations in proposed Pakistan (38% in the North-West and 48% in the North- East)

• Communal self-determination could lead to the separation of Hindu-majority western Bengal and Sikh- and Hindu-dominated Ambala and Jullundur divisions of Punjab.

• Regional ties, economic, administrative, and armed forces division issues were identified.

• **Section-A:** Hindu-majority provinces (Madras, Bombay, Central Provinces, United Provinces, Bihar, and Orissa).

• **Section-B:** Muslim-majority provinces (Punjab, North-West Frontier Province, and Sindh).

• **Section-C:** Muslim-majority provinces (Bengal and Assam).

• Provincial, section, and union levels were established.

• Princely states were no longer under British paramountcy.

• Free to engage with successor governments or the British government.

• Provinces were free to exit groups after general elections.

• After 10 years, provinces can seek a reconsideration of the group or union constitution.

• Interim government to be formed from the constituent assembly.

• The **Muslim League on June 6** and the **Congress on June 24, 1946** accepted the plan.

• **July 1946:** Elections held in provincial assemblies for the Constituent Assembly.

• **July 10, 1946:** Nehru emphasizes that the Constituent Assembly is sovereign, implying the authority to decide rules of procedure.

• **July 29, 1946:** The Muslim League withdrew acceptance of the long-term plan and gave the call for "direct action" from August 16 to achieve Pakistan in response to Nehru's statement.

• **From August 16, 1946**, unprecedented communal riots erupted, causing several thousand deaths.

• Worst-hit areas included Calcutta, Bombay, Noakhali, Bihar, and Garhmukteshwar (United Provinces).

4.17: Independence with Partition

Attlee's Statement

Clement Attlee, the British Prime Minister, made an announcement on February 20, 1947, declaring the British intention to leave the Indian subcontinent.

• Set a **deadline of June 30, 1948**, for the transfer of power, irrespective of the Indian politicians' agreement on the constitution.

• Powers and obligations concerning princely states would lapse with the transfer of power, without transferring to any successor government in British India.

• Lord Mountbatten would replace Lord Wavell as the viceroy.

Mountbatten Plan

• Legislative Assemblies of Punjab and Bengal would vote for partition into separate Hindu and Muslim groups. A simple majority in either group would lead to the partition of these provinces.

• In the case of partition, two dominions (India and Pakistan) and two constituent assemblies would be created. Sindh would make its own decision regarding partition.

• Referendums in NWFP and Sylhet district of Bengal would determine the fate of these areas.

• As Congress had conceded a unified India, all their other points would be met, which are:

    ○ Princely states would not be independent but would join either India or Pakistan.

    ○ Independence for Bengal was ruled out.

    ○ Accession of Hyderabad to Pakistan was ruled out (Mountbatten supported Congress on this).

    ○ Freedom to come on August 15, 1947.

    ○ Boundary commission to be set up if partition was to be effected.

• The League's demand for Pakistan was conceded, and the Congress's position on unity was considered to minimize the size of Pakistan.

• Mountbatten's formula aimed to divide India while retaining maximum unity.

4.18: Evolution of Civil Services in India

➤ Cornwallis (Governor General, 1786–93)

• He was the first to bring into existence and organise the civil services.

➤ Wellesley's Role (Governor General, 1798–1805)

• Fort William College was set up in 1800 to train new recruits.

• East India College was established in England in 1806 after the disapproval of Fort William College by the Court of Directors.

Charter Act of 1853 - Ended Company's patronage; and recruitment through open competition.

➤ Indian Civil Service Act of 1861

• Examination held in England in English language, based on classical learning of Greek and Latin.

• Maximum permissible age was gradually reduced.

• In 1863, Satyendra Nath Tagore became the first Indian to qualify for the Indian Civil Service.

➤ Statutory Civil Service

The Statutory Civil Service was established by Lytton in 1878–1879, with one-sixth of the covenanted posts to be filled by Indians from affluent families who are nominated by local governments and approved by the Viceroy and the Secretary of State.

➤ Aitchison Committee

It recommends dropping 'covenanted' and 'uncovenanted,' classification, classification of the civil service into Imperial Indian Civil Service (examination in England), Provincial Civil Service (examination in India), and Subordinate Civil Service (examination in India); and raising the age limit to 23.

➤ Montford Reforms 1919

• It recommended holding simultaneous exams in India and England.

• one-third of recruitments be made in India itself—to be raised annually by 1.5 per cent.

➤ Lee Commission (1924)

• Secretary of State should continue to recruit ICS; the Irrigation branch of the Service of Engineers, the Indian Forest Service, etc.

• Recruitment for transferred fields like education etc, be made by provincial governments.

• Direct recruitment to ICS on the basis of 50:50 parity between the Europeans and the Indians be reached in 15 years.

• Establishment of Public Service Commission.

➤ Government of India Act, 1935

Recommended Federal and Provincial Public Service Commissions.

4.19: Agrarian Impact of British Policies

Warren Hasting's Revenue System (1769-70)

• He adopted the Izaredari System (also called the farming system) to bring order to revenue collection.

• Contractors selected on the basis of bidding system, given the right to collect revenue for five years. Later it was made annual in 1777.

• Extortion and Oppression by contractors focused on profit, and disregarded peasants' welfare.

• Traditional zamindars were discouraged from bidding. As a result, many hereditary zamindars were removed.

Permanent Settlement

• **Philip Francis** (member of Hastings' council) proposed a permanent land revenue settlement in 1776.

• **Lord Cornwallis** was sent as governor-general with instructions for permanent land revenue settlements with zamindars.

• He set up a committee with himself, Sir John Shore, and James Grant to examine the issue.

• It covered approximately 19% of the territory under British rule and was introduced in Bengal and Bihar, and extended to Orissa, Banaras (Varanasi), and northern Madras.

• Zamindars were given proprietary rights over their land. In 1790, ten-year settlement was made, followed by permanency in 1793.

• Fixed tax imposed on land, collected by zamindars from cultivators (ryots).

• Zamindars were allowed to keep one-tenth to one-eleventh of revenue; the rest was given to the Company government.

• Land Ownership Rights were given to zamindars as they could sell, mortgage, or transfer land; inheritance rights were established.

• A Sunset clause introduced in 1794 made zamindari rights conditional upon tax paid by zamindar.

Ryotwari System

• **Thomas Munro** and **Captain Alexander Read** introduced the system in 1792 in the Baramahal region of Madras Presidency.

• He formalized Ryotwari System in 1820, which extended to various areas in Madras Presidency, excluding those under permanent settlement.

• The system was designed to maximize revenue by collecting directly from villages without intermediaries

• The ownership and occupancy rights were vested in ryots. There was no limit on land ownership; free to sublet, transfer, or sell.

• There was a direct tax payment to the Company (45-55% based on estimated production).

• It was a non-permanent settlement with periodic revision.

• Barren land under government control could be cultivated on the condition of shared revenue.

• Land was confiscated for non-payment.

• Peasants faced arbitrary tax fines, often based on previous payments. High Taxes set at one-third of the gross produce, often equal to economic rental, causing poverty among peasants.

• Ryots coerced and tortured to extract revenue, leading to bondage to the moneylenders.

• A scientific land survey (1855) was initiated, and fresh assessment was undertaken, reducing the actual burden of the tax.

• Reformed Settlement (1864) revenue rate was set at half of the net value of the produce for thirty years.

• Prosperity and Agriculture extension led to agricultural prosperity despite famines in 1865-66 and 1876-78.

Mahalwari System (1819-1822)

• **Holt Mackenzie** recommended it for land revenue settlement in Northern India in 1819.

• Complex survey methods, high revenue demands, and harsh extraction methods lead to a breakdown of the scheme.

• The Agricultural Depression of 1828 worsened it.

Features

• Mahal (village or group of villages) was the basis for revenue assessment.

• Revenue determined was based on the production of a mahal.

• The village community was considered as the owner of the land, while individual ownership was with the cultivator.

• Responsibility for collection and payment lies with the village headman or community of leaders.

• Under Bentinck, the state's revenue share was initially 66%, later modified to 50%.

• The concept of average rents for different soil classes was introduced and land revenue was revised periodically.

• The requirement to record all rights and fix tax on every piece of land was impractical.

• Official calculations are often inaccurate, based on guesswork, and manipulated for increased revenue.

• The system ruined village communities with exorbitant tax assessments.

• The inability to meet tax rates lead to large-scale dispossession, with lands going to moneylenders and merchants.

4.20: Evolution of Press in India

In **1780, James Augustus Hickey** pioneered Indian journalism by establishing **The Bengal Gazette**, the <u>country's first newspaper</u>. Its bold criticism of the government led to its seizure in 1782.

• A wave of newspapers and journals emerged, including The Bengal Journal, **The Calcutta Chronicle, The Madras Courier**, and The **Bombay Herald**, causing anxiety among the East India Company's officers.

• **Raja Rammohan Roy protested** against press freedom restrictions in 1824. The nationalist movement from 1870 to 1918 utilized the press for political propaganda and education.

• Newspapers like **The Hindu, Bengalee, and Amrita Bazar Patrika** played crucial roles. Nationalist newspapers were seen as serving the nation by stimulating the library movement and fostering political education and participation.

• Journalists like **G. Subramania Aiyar, Dadabhai Naoroji, and Bal Gangadhar Tilak** contributed to the press's significance.

Regulations and Press Evolution

➤ **Censorship of Press Act, 1799**

Lord Wellesley enacted <u>stringent press restrictions</u>, anticipating a French invasion. Almost wartime press regulations, including pre-censorship, were imposed.

Lord Hastings later relaxed these restrictions and in 1818, pre-censorship was dispensed with.

➤ Licensing Regulations, 1823

Enacted by **John Adams** (acting governor general), these regulations penalized starting or using a press without a license. Initially directed primarily against Indian-language newspapers or those edited by Indians. Rammohan Roy's Mirat-ul-Akbar had to stop publication.

➤ Press Act of 1835 Or Metcalfe Act

As Governor-General, **Metcalfe repealed the 1823 ordinance** and earned the title "Liberator of the Indian Press." It mandated precise accounts of publication premises and the option to cease functioning if required.

➤ Licensing Act, 1857

Emerged due to the 1857 revolt, imposing licensing restrictions in addition to existing registration procedures. The government reserved the right to stop publication and circulation.

➤ Registration Act, 1867

Replaced Metcalfe's Act and focused on regulation rather than restriction.

Required printing the name of the printer, publisher, and place of the publication, and submitting a copy to the local government within a month from the date of publication of a book.

➤ Vernacular Press Ac t(VPA), 1878

• It aimed to better control the vernacular press and curb "seditious writing" in publications in oriental languages.

• It empowered District Magistrate, which could force printers and publishers to enter bonds, forbidding content that could incite disaffection or antipathy; unappealable Actions and their decisions were final, with no right of appeal in a court of law; government Censorship on vernacular newspapers could seek exemption by submitting proofs to a government censor; the printer and publisher could also be required to deposit security, which could be forfeited if the regulations were contravened, and press equipment could be seized if the offence re-occurred.

• It discriminated between English and vernacular press so, dubbed as the "Gagging Act,". Notably, there was no right of appeal under the VPA.

• The Amrita Bazar Patrika turned overnight into an English newspaper to escape the VPA.

• Later, the pre-censorship clause was repealed, and a press commissioner was appointed to supply authentic and accurate news to the press. Widespread protests led to its repeal by Lord Ripon in 1882.

➤ Newspaper (Incitement to Offences) Act, 1908

It targeted extremist nationalist activities, allowing magistrates to confiscate press property publishing objectionable material likely to cause incitement to murder/acts of violence.

➤ Indian Press Act, 1910

It revived VPA features, empowering local governments to demand security and submit copies of newspapers free of charge.

➤ Defence of India Rules (First World War)

It was imposed for political repression and criticism. Based on the Press Committee's recommendations chaired by Tej Bahadur Sapru, the Press Acts of 1908 and 1910 were repealed.

➤ Indian Press (Emergency Powers) Act, 1931

It gave sweeping powers to provincial governments to suppress propaganda for the Civil Disobedience Movement. It was further amplified in 1932 to include all activities calculated to undermine government authority.

➤ Defence of India Rules (Second World War)

Pre-censorship was imposed, and amendments were made to the Press Emergency Act and Official Secrets Act. At one time, publication of all news related to Congress activity was declared illegal.

4.21: Important Congress Session

Year	Place	President	Details
1885	Bombay	W.C. Banerjee	1st session, attended by 72 delegates
1886	Calcutta	Dadabhai Naoroji	Witnessed merger of INC and National Conference

1887	Madras	Bdruddin Tyabji	Appeal to Muslims to join INC.
1888	Allahabad	Gorge Yule	1st non-Indian President of INC.
1896	Calcutta	Rahimatullah M. Sayani	National song "Vande Mataram" sung for the first time.
1905	Benaras	Gopal Krishna Gokhale	Resentment against the Bengal partition, boycott of foreign goods, promotion of Swadeshi goods and Indian industries, public meetings, and processions
1906	Calcutta	Dadabhai Naoroji	Word Swaraj mentioned for the first time.
1907	Surat	Rash Behari Ghosh	Congress split between moderates and extremists
1908	Madras	Rash Behari Ghosh	The Constitution of INC drawn
1909	Lahore	Madan Mohan Malviya	Disapproval of separate electorates based on religion (Indian Councils Act, 1909).
1911	Calcutta	Bishan Narayan Dar	National Anthem, "Jana Gana Mana," sung for the first time
1916	Lucknow	A.C. Majumdar	Reunification of Moderates and Extremists in INC, Lucknow Pact between Muslim League and INC, Death of Gokhale and Pherozshah Mehta
1917	Calcutta	Annie Besant	First woman to preside the Congress session.
1919	Amritsar	Motinal Nehru	New constitution of INC framed, Condemned the Jallianwala Bagh massacre, Approved the Khilafat movement

1920	Calcutta	Lala Lajpat Rai	**Special Session.** NCM moved and adopted.
1920	Nagpur	C. Vijayaragha vachariar	Reconstitution of Congress committees on linguistic grounds
1922	Gaya	C.R. Das	CR Das and other leaders broke away from INC and formed the Swaraj party. CR Das presided over the session when he was in jail
1923	Delhi	Maulana Azad	Maulana Abul Kalam Azad became the youngest president of INC.
1924	Belgaum	M. K. Gandhi	Only session where Gandhiji presided
1925	Kanpur	Sarojini Naidu	First Indian women president of INC
1927	Madras	M. A. Ansari	Resolution against using Indian troops in Mesopotamia, Iran, and China. The resolution passed to boycott the Simon Commission.
1928	Calcutta	Motilal Nehru	1st All India Youth Congress Formed.
1929	Lahore	Jawaharlal Nehru	Adopted resolution for Purna Swaraj
1931	Karachi	Vallabh Bhai Patel	Endorsed Gandhi Irwin pact, Resolution of Fundamental rights and National Economic Programme
1934	Bombay	Rajendra Prasad	INC Constitution amended
1936	Faizpur	Jawaharlal Nehru	Push towards socialist ideas by Nehru, 1st session in a village
1938	Haripura	Subhas Chandra Bose	National Planning Committee set under Nehru

1939	Tripuri	Subhas Chnadra Bose	Rajendra Prasad took over as president after Subhas Chandra resigned.
1940	Ramgarh	Maulana Abul Kalam Azad	The decision to take the final call on launching mass civil disobedience was left to Mahatma Gandhi.
1946	Meerut	Acharya J.B. Kripalani	Last Session before Independence.

Recently, the **<u>Kaziranga National Park and Tiger Reserve</u>** in **Assam** has received the **addition of two new mammalian species**, the elusive binturong (Arctictis binturong) and the small-clawed otter.